Praise

THOUGHT
ECONOMICS

'If you value those who think differently, read *Thought Economics*. Challenging traditional thought structure is what it's all about. I'm so glad this book exists.' Rose McGowan, author of *Brave*

'The remarkable thing about *Thought Economics* is that it isn't just thought-provoking, but genuinely thought-generating. It is a watershed in our understanding, and our understanding of understanding. Vikas Shah hasn't just moved the needle, he's fashioned an exciting new one.' Dexter Dias QC, author of *The Ten Types of Human*

'A must-read collection of interviews with incredible people – and also me.' David Baddiel

'It's a joy to dip in and out of these learnings and insights.' Sophia Amoruso, author of *#Girlboss*

'An incredible collection of interviews with the people that have shaped our world.' Heston Blumenthal

THOUGHT ECONOMICS

**conversations with the remarkable
people shaping our century**

VIKAS SHAH

Michael O'Mara Books Limited

First published in Great Britain in 2021
by Michael O'Mara Books Limited
9 Lion Yard
Tremadoc Road
London SW4 7NQ

A CIP catalogue record for this book is available from the British Library.

Papers used by Michael O'Mara Books Limited are natural, recyclable
products made from wood grown in sustainable forests. The manufacturing
processes conform to the environmental regulations of the country of origin.

ISBN: 978-1-78929-245-9 in hardback print format
ISBN: 978-1-78929-315-9 in trade paperback print format
ISBN: 978-1-78929-267-1 in ebook format

1 2 3 4 5 6 7 8 9 10

www.mombooks.com

Designed and typeset by Design 23

Printed and bound by CPI Group (UK) Ltd, Croydon, CR0 4YY

CONTENTS

Acknowledgements   8
Foreword by Lemn Sissay   9
Introduction   13

1. On Identity: Who We Are   19

Marina Abramović, Professor Jim Al-Khalili, Professor Kwame Anthony Appiah, Professor Justin Barrett, Professor Sean Carroll, Professor Deepak Chopra, Professor George Church, Dame Jane Morris Goodall DBE, Sir Antony Gormley, Bear Grylls OBE, Professor Yuval Noah Harari, Sir Anish Kapoor CBE, Rose McGowan, Sam Neill, Dr Jordan B. Peterson, Professor Steven Pinker, Sir Ken Robinson, Professor Carlo Rovelli, Sadhguru, Dr Carl Safina, Dr Elif Shafak, Philippe Starck, Professor Jack Szostak

2. On Culture: The Context of Humanity   51

Dr Maya Angelou, David Bailey CBE, Black Thought, Heston Blumenthal OBE, Ed Catmull, Alain Ducasse, Tracey Emin CBE, George the Poet, Paul Greengrass, Siddharth Roy Kapur, Lang Lang, Ken Loach, Yann Martel, Moby, Sir Andrew Motion, Rankin, Dr Elif Shafak, Ritesh Sidhwani, Lemn Sissay MBE, Saul Williams, Hans Zimmer

3. On Leadership: Bringing Humanity Together   92

Carlo Ancelotti OSI, Mark Cuban, Professor Stew Friedman, Professor Green, Colonel Chris Hadfield, Gary Hamel, Tony Hsieh, Arianna Huffington, Professor John Kotter, General Stanley McChrystal, General Richard Myers, Jacqueline Novogratz, Professor Robert Bernard Reich, Nico Rosberg, Sheryl Sandberg, Stephen Schwarzman, General Sir Richard Shirreff KCB CBE, Hamdi Ulukaya, Jocko Willink

4. On Entrepreneurship: The Creators and the Makers   128

Sophia Amoruso, Steve Ballmer, Sir Richard Branson, Tory Burch, Stewart Butterfield, Steve Case, Dennis Crowley, Sir James Dyson, Jamal Edwards MBE, Tony O. Elumelu, Scott Farquhar, Naveen Jain, Donna Karan, Robin Li, Kiran Mazumdar-Shaw, N. R. Narayana Murthy, José Neves, Kevin O'Leary, Professor Michael Otto, Gary Vaynerchuk, Jack Welch, will.i.am, Chip Wilson, Jerry Yang, Professor Muhammad Yunus

5. On Discrimination and Injustice: Them and Us   168

David Baddiel, Laura Bates, Lord John Bird MBE, Sir Philip Craven MBE, F. W. de Klerk, Dexter Dias QC, Melinda Gates, Leymah Gbowee, Matt Haig, Afua Hirsch, Baroness Ruth Hunt, Jameela Jamil, L. A. Kauffman, Iby Knill BEM, Rose McGowan, Dr Gad Saad, Harry Leslie Smith, George Takei, Peter Tatchell, Ai Weiwei

6. On Conflict: War, Peace and Justice   208

Bertie Ahern, Martti Ahtisaari, Professor Zeid Ra'ad Al Hussein, Professor Alexander Betts, Marina Cantacuzino, Professor François Crépeau, Dr Shirin Ebadi, Ben Ferencz, Gulwali Passarlay, Professor George Rupp, Lech Wałęsa, Jody Williams, Catherine Woollard

7. On Democracy: A 2,500-year   240
Experiment in Power

Alastair Campbell, Noam Chomsky, Vicente Fox Quesada, Professor A. C. Grayling, Susan Herman, Toomas Hendrik Ilves, Garry Kasparov, Michael Lewis, Ted Lieu, Moisés Naím, Admiral James Stavridis, Ece Temelkuran, Yanis Varoufakis, Guy Verhofstadt, Lord Woolf, Bassem Youssef

Index   277

ACKNOWLEDGEMENTS

To my incredible wife, Rachael Shah, who is my biggest cheerleader and has always pushed me to follow my heart. To Danny Donachie, who planted the seed of this idea a decade ago, sitting on a roof terrace with a cup of tea. To Lesley O'Mara, Jo Stansall and the team at Michael O'Mara Books for supporting and guiding me through this process; to Joel Cohen and Hayley Olsen, who have edited, corrected and reviewed my interviews since 2007; and to Luke Bainbridge, whose journalistic eye helped to refine so much of this work.

To every single interviewee who has given up the most precious commodity they have – time – to speak to me.

Thank you.

FOREWORD

BY LEMN SISSAY

Nomenclature and Thought Economics. A title needs to be unique to avoid the search-engine crash of discovering it corresponds with an obscure naked yoga cult in northern Kazakhstan. Vikas's Thought Economics website was original from the start and its name serves as the first unique phrase in this entire project. You have chosen well.

As I am writing this, the United Kingdom is in lockdown. Previous to the pandemic, 'lockdown' was a description of cell-bound prisoners. 'Lockdown' enabled officers to search the cells, one by one, for contraband. Now we are in lockdown in our own homes, searching ourselves, one by one. Meanwhile, Covid-19 prowls across the globe with scant regard for boundaries and no respect for governments, for organizations, for us. The virus as terrorist, cloaked in invisibility, wreaks havoc wherever it is. We place ourselves indoors to protect ourselves, we wear masks – and we are faced, most of all, with ourselves. It is up to us. Our thoughts. Our economics.

Resilience is needed. Hope is needed. Family is needed. Business is needed. The arts are needed. Government is needed. Friends are needed. All are represented in these pages. Their value appreciates with need. We see more clearly what is precious, that which should be maintained and that which must be jettisoned. 'I hope that everyone could wake up in the morning and wonder what their purpose is. This is the main question of our existence!' (Marina Abramović).

But there is a gift in lockdown, a gift to governments and societies of the world. We have experienced now what happens when we place the wellbeing of fellow humans above profit and war. Another advantage to lockdown is The Book as a source of solace. The paper book is regaining its rightful place in tandem with the screen. On the arrival of the internet two decades ago, the book faced its greatest challenge. Today, there are more words passing between more people than *ever*. It was at the beginning of this revolution that the Thought Economics blog came to fruition.

In this book, Vikas converses with some of the most inspiring minds on the planet. It is an intimate and expansive expedition into what happens when a good question is asked of a great mind. Page after page of cross-thinking and counterintuitive insight. Through his questions, Vikas draws the brightest minds into seven chapters. Here, for example, in Chapter 7, chess master Garry Kasparov talks about democracy:

> More and more young people are getting interested in politics, and we should praise Trump for waking them up. Democracy is not something that is granted for ever. Ronald Reagan once said, 'Freedom is never more than one generation away from extinction,' and our democratic instruments have got rusty, as people assumed they would always work automatically.

So a Russian chess master quotes a past American president to describe what is happening in the world today. It reminds me of the dynamism in Matthew Syed's *Rebel Ideas*, in which he encourages different sources of thought for the boardroom to stimulate innovative ideas. Likewise, this book is fizzing with ideas for the boardroom, and for you. There is an urgency to *Thought Economics* that perfectly matches our times. The chapter headings say it all.

I am proud to say that Vikas Shah is a friend. Oftentimes I would call him and he would say, 'Can't talk now, got an interview.' A week or so later I'd receive the interview in my inbox. It could be a conversation with Arianna Huffington, or the world's richest philanthropist, Melinda Gates. The list is jaw-dropping: Nobel prizewinners, record producers, global artists, particle physicists, prime ministers. 'How do you get these incredible interviewees?' I'd ask him. 'I phone them,' is his response. And then the penny drops. He gets incredible interviews because he's an incredible guy.

If the art of the question is without question an art, then Vikas is Picasso. When a critic said to Picasso that he couldn't paint a tree, it is alleged Picasso replied, 'He's right. I can't paint a tree, but I can paint the feeling you have when you look at a tree.' Vikas draws such detail from his interviewees. No stone is unturned. The prime minister answers a question next to the artist. The insights within the answers stay with you. And then there is the simple pleasure of hearing masters of their craft like filmmaker Paul Greengrass speak about why they make art:

> There is a beauty to the collective experience of going to the cinema. The great David Lean used to say that when he was a boy, and went to the cinema, he looked at the beam of light coming down towards the screen as if it were the light coming through a cathedral window; it gave him a pious sensation – and there's something to that. Cinema has a mystery, a magic.

I liken *Thought Economics* to the *Paris Review*. Read this book. Keep it for years. The wisdom in it will stay with you for life. Whether you are a CEO or the cleaner where the CEO works, there is something in here for you, something that could change your life, something that could encourage you to keep going in the direction you are going. There is no pretension here. The interviews are easy to read and, above all, nourishing. Right now, *Thought Economics* is a vital addition to our world.

INTRODUCTION

I have no business writing this book. I'm neither a journalist, nor a professional writer. What I am, however, is curious. I was the kid who kept asking questions in class, the one who tracked teachers down while they were on their well-earned breaks to ask nice simple questions like, 'So, how does the universe work?'

My day job is in the world of business, and I guess you could call me an entrepreneur. But I don't want to unnecessarily glamorize it by making you think of shiny people getting out of shiny private planes into shiny cars, checking the time on their house-priced shiny watches, before passing the big shiny gate of their gigantic architect-designed home. That's not me. My companies are all firmly part of the small-business world.

The reason for my profile is more to do with the journey than the numbers. I started my first business when I was fourteen, which probably seems quite old by today's tech-entrepreneur standards, but back then it was considered quite a fresh-faced age to be in the cut-and-thrust world of enterprise. That business, Ultima Group, was in web design and software development, but we also had a little side hustle called *Independent Software Reviews*. This was one of the first online magazines, and my colleagues and I reviewed computer games, software and music. We didn't realize how early we were to the table as an online publication, and before long this side-hustle gained momentum and we were receiving over half a million unique users per month. Back in the early days of the internet this was a huge number. We built one of the world's first content management systems (which we called the 'flatpack web') and syndicated content around the world. I suspect one of the only reasons we didn't capitalize more on the success of this publication was that we were all kids. This business (and the publication) came to an abrupt halt as the first dotcom bubble burst in 2001, but the writing bug never quite left me.

My generation was perhaps the last to be habituated with long-form content; we grew up with newspapers, journals and books, rather than the omnichannel video, podcast and social formats that became the norm by the start of this century. We also saw the world shift rapidly as technology gained prominence in our economic, cultural and social transactions and ideas became visibly the new engine of power. We have always talked about markets, the economy, culture, society and politics as phenomena that exist outside ourselves, when, in fact, they are the product of ideas, of people. They are not apart from us; they *are* us. That was my 'aha' moment, though it took some time to brew.

Fast-forward to the year 2007. Combining a need to fix my frustration at the lack of long-form content and my desire to write, I created a blog. It didn't even have a domain – it was simply thoughteconomics.blogspot.com, a very simple blog without any design templates on Google's free blogging platform. The name Thought Economics was born of the fact that it was thinking, ideas, concepts – the products of thought – that create our world, and so perhaps my blog could explore that. My plan was simply to publish the occasional long-form article myself on a topic of interest and include interviews with interesting people I'd met or got to know over the years. There was no strategy here – it was simply a way of indulging a hobby alongside my day job(s). I didn't want to editorialize or turn the interviews into opinion pieces, but rather I transcribed the conversations and posted them as they were.

The more interviews I posted, the more the traffic grew, and it quickly became apparent that there was an audience out there who really enjoyed long-form interview content in a way that was raw, unedited and (quite importantly) not behind a paywall. By 2008, I'd started to regularly get emails from readers all over the world suggesting topics and individuals they would like me to approach – and that's really where I returned to that aha moment. I made a pivot (to steal the start-up parlance) – I bought the domain thoughteconomics.com, built a proper website (albeit in WordPress) and began my mission to capture interviews with the individuals who I felt had made a meaningful impact in our time.

One of my first big-name interviews was with Jimmy Wales (founder of Wikipedia), and this experience taught me an important lesson: be more prepared. Jimmy was the first household name to grant my humble little blog their time. I sent him the questions I wanted to ask, and his response was quite simple: 'I've answered those all before, try again.' From that point on, I committed not only to research every interviewee in more detail, but to work with them to prepare questions around the areas they were most passionate about, and most interested in.

Rather miraculously, and only a few months later, I had a call booked with one of my personal heroes, former astronaut Buzz Aldrin. I'd done some pretty nerve-wracking things in my career thus far, but here I was, early evening UK time, waiting by the phone in my office for Buzz Aldrin to call me. The interview went well, but towards the end a particularly memorable moment reminded me that I was doing something quite unusual. My dad was in the office, as we had planned to get dinner together that evening and, mid-interview, he came over to me:

> Dad: Do you want a cup of tea?
> Me: (Hits mute on the phone.) No thanks, Dad, I'm a bit busy here ...
> Dad: Who are you on the phone to?
> Me: Buzz Aldrin.
> Dad: Bollocks. (Laughs as he walks back to the kitchen.)

I'd almost lost sight of how incredible these opportunities were in the excitement of growing my new website, but the disbelief my friends and family had about who I was speaking to made me realize what an absolute privilege it is to be able to get one-to-one time on the phone with some of the most influential and interesting people on the planet.

After I'd published my interview with Buzz, a journalist from a major newspaper emailed me and asked, 'So, how did you get hold of him? We've been trying for a long time.' I get asked this a lot, and my honest reply is that I just don't know. I just asked! Of course, for every interview I publish, what you don't see is the slew of rejections. I would estimate that every interview I get is the product of at least twenty approaches, and hence nineteen rejections. Sometimes it can feel personal – in the process of writing this book, I reached out to one leadership expert in the USA, and his office replied, 'Aren't most of the interviews on your site fake? I'm sorry, this doesn't pass muster.' A pretty god-awful reply, which can trigger a whole host of emotions, until I remind myself that I'm approaching people who get asked for interviews constantly, individuals who have a natural guard up and also who will have layers of people around them, primarily to protect and defend their time. In many ways, Thought Economics has been an exercise in determination for me, to prove to people that it is possible to do absurdly ambitious things if you have the tenacity and resilience.

When I was approached by my publishers about turning some of my conversations into a book, I worked through some of my favourite interviews and was struck by the common themes that ran through a lot of my questions and their revealing answers. The first was identity and the eternal question of who we are, what our purpose is, and what our place is in the world. This also led to many questions about culture, the paste that binds us together – our art, our music, our literature, everything that's really important and feeds into our ideas on identity and belonging. That notion of belonging extends to those fundamental biases we carry in our own society. Discrimination in all its forms has resulted in pain, suffering and inequalities through the choices we have made about who is in or out of our tribes and groups – and has often been the cause of the conflicts we have seen as a backdrop to most of human history. Alongside these obvious challenges, society has made huge progress in peacebuilding and the greatest governance experiment of our times, democracy, which has created the political, legal and economic framework on which entrepreneurs have created the innovations, ideas and businesses that have pushed our world forward, creating a backbone for our economy, providing employment, opportunity and solving many of our most pressing challenges. All of this, however, would be impossible without leadership, and in every single interview I have done, it is those leadership qualities – the ability to inspire, to pull people together, and achieve the impossible – that have shone through.

Without a doubt, there are gaps within these chapters. There will be major topics or individuals you feel are missing; there may be perspectives that have not been addressed, or truths that need to be told. Thought Economics is constantly evolving, and interviews are being added regularly. I'm passionate about diversity of thought and perspectives, and will always do my best to make sure that it is represented across the site.

The best and worst of humanity has come as a result of our ideas, and at a time when so much of our world is feeling culturally, socially, economically and politically unstable, it's on all of us not only to talk openly and honestly about these issues, but to take in as much diverse knowledge and as many opinions as we can, in a bid to understand them more deeply, rather than simply skim-reading enough to troll each other on Twitter.

It is in the spirit of creating that depth of understanding that I am committing a minimum of £10,000 of the royalties from this book to two organizations: In Place of War, an international charity I chair, which works across thirty countries in communities impacted by conflict, using the arts, research and entrepreneurship to build sustainable peace and opportunity; and the University of Manchester, England's first civic university, closely linked to Manchester's development as the world's first industrial city, and a place that is carrying out world-changing research in many important areas. Both of these are charitable organizations, and both are fighting for knowledge, the power of thought, to be the light that shows us ways to change the world.

It is an honour to share these conversations with you, and if you want to share your feedback, or have suggestions for any new interviews or topics, you are always welcome to email me: vs@thoughteconomics.com, or tweet @MrVikas.

Vikas Shah MBE
July 2020, London
www.thoughteconomics.com

ON IDENTITY: WHO WE ARE

'Reality is not a collection of objects with properties: it is a network of interactions and relative information.'

CARLO ROVELLI

Who are you? Well, physically, you're mainly a bag of water. That sounds unremarkable enough, until you realize that the amount of water on our planet has remained reasonably constant since earth was formed about 4.5 billion years ago. Thus you, me and everyone around us are big bags of ancient water, which has cycled through oceans, rivers, forests and between each other. You could also be described as a bag of stuff, of matter, of atoms. Again, that sounds unremarkable enough until you realize that the stuff that forms us was made deep in the heart of stars, billions of years ago and, through processes that we still don't fully understand, came to form you and me – strange super-monkeys that are intelligent enough to contemplate their origin and place in the universe.

Even the fundamental question of what we are when we refer to 'I' is fraught with doubt. Every day our body is changing and regenerating physically and developing mentally. It's unlikely, for example, that you have many cells in your body now that were present at your birth, and the connections in your brain will be vastly different today than even a decade ago. When we refer to the self, we are really talking of the experiential continuity that has brought us to this present moment. You are in effect the result of your own idiosyncratic path through the gamut of reality, and the fact that those experiences are unique to you creates the self as an individual that exists as a phenomenon in time, irrespective and apart from any other individual. Understanding the self in this way is important. You are a unique and beautiful living experiment that is conscious enough to observe itself. The experiment of you is informed by a constant process of learning, given context by our education. To put it another way: we live, we learn. And that last point – learning – is critical. For most of history, deep thinking and self-discovery were tasks largely left to the intelligentsia and those who ruled their domain, whether it be religion, politics or nobility. The rest of us had to be passive and obedient enough to be useful, and relatively predictable.

As our species has progressed technologically, however, it has also become ever more protean. A citizen is no longer defined by 'what' they do, but rather exists as an individual who is able to learn, to question and to grow. Our new diffuse culture has also created the opportunity for humanity to innovate; we can explore who we are and what we are capable of in more dramatic ways than could ever be imagined. In the 1950s, for example, it would have been impossible to conceive the total sum of human knowledge being contained within a human-made computer network, or that we would have the technology to decode our very DNA, or that billions could be educated digitally in communities that still lack basic access to food and water. But less than half a century later, those things are taken for granted. The pace of change socially, culturally and technologically in our world is increasing rapidly, meaning that the shape of humanity even a decade from now will be significantly different to today, and invariably will require a different set of cognitive, emotional and spiritual apparatus to that which we currently wield.

Identity and who we are is so key to how we view everything else in our world that I wanted to start this book here. In this chapter are some of the conversations I had with artists, whose work naturally seeks to explain our place in the world. It also contains parts of some of the interviews I conducted with spiritual leaders for whom faith is a shared narrative of our experience of humanity, and with academics whose research and study are helping us to understand the beginnings of life itself. I have also included some of my interviews with leading physicists, who spoke to me about our place in the universe. Understanding identity, however, would feel incomplete without delving into the stories of our time, and so I'd also like to share conversations I had with some inspirational writers, who gave deeply beautiful accounts of who we are.

Why do identities matter?

Kwame Anthony Appiah: Identities essentially involve a few key elements. We have a label with ideas about how to apply it – to others, and by others. The label gives us a way to think, feel and do things and also consequences for identifying and thinking under that label. We also have the reality that in a society, the label affects how other people treat you and shapes how you treat and see them. For those of us who have an identity, it offers a conception of who we are, and helps us to think about how we ought to behave, who we belong with, with whom we should have solidarity, with whom we have conflict and who is on the inside and outside. Some of this, of course, can lead to negative outcomes, but there is a positive role of identity in shaping who we are. Modern life has allowed more identities, with more packages of expectations and behaviours for people who have those identities. In modern society, too, we can reject labels altogether and say, 'I'm not a man! I'm a woman!' or 'I am a man, but being a man doesn't have to be like that, it can be like this ...'

How can we find our identity in this world?

Elif Shafak: I have always been very critical of identity politics. It saddens me to see how within my side of the political spectrum – the liberal left in general – many people, especially young people, want to defend identity politics as a progressive force. It is not. Identity politics can be a good starting point to raise awareness, but it cannot be our destination, it cannot be where we end up. The answer to a tribal instinct is not to retreat into another tribe. The way forward is to challenge the very mentality of tribalism. When I examine myself, I can see clearly that I do not have an identity. Instead I have multiple belongings. I am an Istanbulite, and I will carry Istanbul with me wherever I go. I am attached to the Aegean, the other side of the water, so Greek culture is also close to my heart. I am attached to Anatolia, with all its traditions and cultures: Armenian, Sephardic, Alevi, Kurdish, Turkish, Yazidi. I'll embrace them all. I am attached to the Balkans – Bulgarian, Romanian, Serbian, Slavic. I am attached to the Middle East: put me next to someone from Lebanon, Iran, Egypt, Iraq – I have so much to share with them. At the same time, I am a European by birth, by choice, in the core values that I uphold. I am a Londoner, a British citizen and a citizen of the world, and a global soul. I am a mother, a writer, a storyteller, a woman, a nomad, a mystic, but also an agnostic, a bisexual, a feminist. Just like Walt Whitman said, 'I contain multitudes.' We all contain multitudes.

How have identities shaped society?

Kwame Anthony Appiah: Class has the virtue of being a kind of social identity that's tied to something objectively real, that being your socioeconomic options. In some ways, our societies are becoming increasingly economically polarized and one of the challenges for those doing well out of the system (the club classes) is to distract people from the power of identity because if people organized around class identity, they would presumably be deposed since those at the bottom of the hierarchy are larger in number, and presumably they would wish to take action to reduce inequality. It's a puzzle to me why class doesn't play a bigger role in our politics. We use identities to make ourselves, to define ourselves with and against people – and we have to make a conscious effort to see this, else we will over-assign significance to identity, as we do in the world of gender. Women and men are far more similar than our gender ideologies suggest to us and we've been trying very hard for a couple of generations to push against the bad consequences of gender discrimination and patriarchy (the gender parallel to white supremacy). We've been trying to drive it out of our system, but people keep falling back into it. You cannot get rid of identities, but you can reform them.

Why do so many people build identity just on what they do?

Rose McGowan: I remember coming to a point where I realized that just because someone has a business card with their occupation on, it doesn't define who they are or actually what they do. Why don't those activities, which you don't get paid for, which are your interests and passions, also qualify as being what you do; and why aren't they, in some ways, more valuable? The two can certainly dovetail, but for most people these 'other' activities are dismissed as hobbies – or 'useless talents' – because they don't make money. Those talents are actually there to help you to define yourself. I want to push society to grow, and four years ago when the #MeToo movement began, that was the idea: to see if we could push at the overall thought structure, and break those conversations that were happening over and over again. It was a bit like a cultural reset.

⚙️⚙️

When people gather, I always think it's interesting to hear the topics of conversation that ensue most often. If someone says, 'So, tell me about yourself,' the natural response is often to start with your occupation – 'I run a business', 'I am a lawyer', 'I am a doctor' and so on. When my first business collapsed following the dotcom bubble bursting, I came to realize very abruptly that defining your identity by what you do is dangerous and also limiting. We are capable of so much more than our jobs, and worth more, too. For as long as we've asked questions, religion and spirituality have been sources of answers, providing comfort and explanation for billions. I was born into quite a religious Hindu household, and saw this first-hand as my parents and extended family turned to religion to provide answers to the challenges of everyday life. As for me, my school, while grounded in faith, as many British schools are, had roots in science and in secular enquiry, and so my entire world view has been framed with this nuanced lens of deep respect for scientific and spiritual answers.

What does it mean to be alive?

Sadhguru: Not everybody is alive to the same extent. Life is available to us in many different dimensions, at different levels of sensitivity and perception, and unfortunately, not everyone is alive to the same extent; and that is why I've dedicated my work to get people to their fullest possible 'aliveness'. The fundamental purpose of life is to know life in its full depth and dimension. If you want to know life, the only way is for you to live your own life at its peak. You are incapable of experiencing anything outside of you. What you think of as light and darkness are within you, that which is pleasure and pain happens within you, agony and ecstasy happen within you. Everything that you ever experience happens within you, and it's your own aliveness that gives you access to the more profound dimensions of life to be experienced.

What does it mean to have a life well lived?

Jordan B. Peterson: A life well lived means that you spend a substantial amount of time addressing the troubles of the world – trouble with yourself, your family, your community. Everyone has a sense that things are less than they could be, and everyone is affected by the suffering they see around them. It seems to me that lays a moral burden on us that can't be avoided, and that the only way to rectify this burden is to confront it and try to do something about it. People inevitably find that the worthwhile things they've done in their life – the things that give them strength and forbearance and a certain amount of self-respect – are acts of responsibility that they have been undertaking in the face of serious problems.

Making happiness the key pursuit in life is just hopeless. It's just not a pursuit that's going to fulfil itself. Life is already complex enough to make us anxious, painful, disappointed and hurt: that's not a pessimistic viewpoint; it's the truth. My experience has been that it takes very little time to talk to someone, so that if you really listen to them and get below the surface, you'll find out how many truly difficult things they're dealing with on a day-to-day-basis. You do see people in rare periods of life where they're comparatively carefree, but that's not common, as far as I'm concerned. The idea that impulsive gratification and 'happiness' are going to rectify life's problems just strikes me as naïve beyond tenability, and so it's no surprise that life is just a constant disappointment for people.

Anish Kapoor: Those moments of full involvement, when you lose yourself, those are moments when you are most alive. There's a moment when you look at good art when time changes. It's as if time no longer exists, becomes longer, or is suspended. There's a moment of reverie when you're fully immersed in something apart from yourself. One experiences this sometimes in meditation. These inexplicable, wonderful and mysterious experiences we have never leave us. I was recently in the desert of Namibia, one of the most beautiful places in the world. In this space, there were a lot of dead animals – carcasses that were just there. Every time I encountered one of these dead animals it made me think, 'This is a good place to die.' Why? Somehow, living and dying bode well in those open, harsh, fundamental spaces.

Sam Neill: I don't expect to be remembered for anything much, if at all. I remember once reading a quote along the lines of, 'you should hope that after you've gone, your name may be a sweet sound on someone's lips …' I thought that's probably about as good as it gets. Films evaporate like everything else and it's culture that decides what is important and what will get remembered.

Why do humans feel a sense of difference from other species?

Yuval Noah Harari: Because we dominate and exploit other species, we need to justify this to ourselves. So we tend to think that we are a superior life form, and that there is a huge gap separating us from all the other animals. This was not always so. Prior to the Agricultural Revolution, hunter-gatherers did not feel very different from other animals. They saw themselves as part and parcel of the natural world, and as constantly communicating and negotiating with the animals, plants and natural phenomena around them. However, once the Agricultural Revolution gave humans power over other animals, they began to see themselves as essentially different. So they invented various religions that elevated humans above the rest of creation. We normally think that religions such as Judaism, Christianity and Islam sanctified the great gods. We tend to forget that they sanctified humans, too. One of God's main jobs is to account for the superiority of man over animal.

How can we find meaning in our lives and a basis for morality?

Steven Pinker: If anything, the belief in God gets in the way of a moral and meaningful life for reasons that go back to the *Euthyphro* by Plato. If one believes in God as the granter of moral truths, one can still ask, 'Well, how did God himself arrive at those moral truths?' and if the arbitrary answer is that they were a whim, or a personal preference of God, why should we therefore take those arbitrary preferences seriously. On the other hand, if God had good reasons for the moral precepts that [he] advances in scripture, why don't we appeal to those precepts directly. The endorsement of a supernatural entity should be irrelevant.

In answering the question of how we make our lives meaningful, we must look at the basis on which we find morality, and that morality ultimately hinges on a notion of impartiality. I cannot argue that my own interests are special and yours are not simply because I'm me and hope that you take me seriously. Finding meaning is different to finding morality, and comes down to recognizing our place in the natural world, our inherent vulnerability, and the many ways in which the laws of nature have no concern for our wellbeing – if anything, they appear to be grinding us down. Finding meaning is also contextualized by the law of entropy – the second law of thermodynamics – that disorder increases without the infusion of energy and information and the process of evolution, which is indifferent to our individual wellbeing. Indeed, it is a competitive process and means that we are always vulnerable to pathogens, parasites, spoilage, organisms and vermin – not to mention our own competitive instincts that lead to humans often becoming their own worst enemy. That is the reality we are born into.

What is 'life' and what does it mean to feel alive?

George Church: Most discussions of 'What is life?' get tangled in assuming a dichotomy, a sharp line sought between life and non-life. In contrast, I favour the idea of a quantitative spectrum of levels of 'life' or 'replicated complexity', with higher levels of such replexity being more alive than merely replicated simple structures like salt, and more alive than arbitrarily random complex structures like fire. To maintain their high replexity life status, these systems 'feel alive'– that is, they typically use senses and responses to deal with potential threats and opportunities. The urge to live is often aimed at supporting survival of offspring around them.

Jack Szostak: We certainly don't fully understand how life emerged on the early earth. One of the most exciting aspects of modern science is that this is now a question we can really get into. People spend a lot of time coming up with a definition of life, which doesn't seem like a fruitful exercise. We don't need to precisely define life in order to study the origin of life; what we need is a pathway that goes from the chemistry of the early earth, to more complex states, and then a transition to simple cells and modern life; in other words, a continuous path from chemistry to modern biology. It's filling in all the steps in that pathway where the interesting problems lie. If you try to simply define the dividing line between life and non-life, you won't really be attacking the important questions.

Can every life have meaning?

Marina Abramović: I hope that everyone could wake up in the morning and wonder what their purpose is. This is the main question of our existence! So many people are lost, taking antidepressants and drinking, and often because they don't want to face this fundamental question, or because they don't have time to face this question. It's often easier to take antidepressants and become a zombie instead of posing this question to yourself. Life is a miracle. It's the most beautiful gift in the world. We're temporary visitors to this planet and we have to be happy. And to be happy, you have to understand that death can come at any moment, at any time. Once you accept that, you see that every moment is precious.

Where do you find joy in life?

Sam Neill: You know when you're happy, you know when you're unhappy, and you know when you're in between, but I think happiness is elusive, especially now. The impact of our current [Covid-19] lockdown has been devastating on people to whom life is already unfair – it's been brutal, and life is changing so fast right now. Whatever we do today will be out of date next week. This business of finding happiness is hard during these dark times.

How can you conquer your fears?

Bear Grylls: Time, experience and a whole bunch of narrow escapes has taught me that the best way over our fears is not to run from them, but to face them and walk right through the middle. This way they often shrink. When we refuse to face stuff, though, then fears tend to escalate. That's the irony. We all have fears; it is what makes us human. But in essence, I try and see how that fear is there to sharpen me, not frighten me. I try and use it to keep those senses alert and ready. It is always present before big adventures, and I guess I have grown a little more used to it – but as a team we never get complacent. It is good to be honest about those fears, as is the case for me with skydiving. Ever since my free-fall accident I have found it hard to do, but it is a key part of my job, and knowing that hand is on my shoulder from one of the crew before I jump always helps me.

What do you fear and hope for the future of our species?

Yuval Noah Harari: To put it bluntly, I think in the future humans will use technology to upgrade themselves into gods. I mean this literally, not metaphorically. Humans are going to acquire abilities that were traditionally thought to be divine abilities. Humans may soon be able to design and create living beings at will, to surf artificial realities directly with their minds, to radically extend their lifespans, and to change their own bodies and minds according to their wishes. Throughout history there were many economic, social and political revolutions. But one thing remained constant:

humanity itself. We still have the same body and mind as our ancestors in the Roman Empire or in ancient Egypt. Yet in the coming decades, for the first time in history, humanity itself will undergo a radical revolution. Not only our society and economy, but our bodies and minds will be transformed by genetic engineering, nanotechnology and brain–computer interfaces. Bodies and minds will be the main products of the twenty-first-century economy. When we think about the future, we generally think about a world in which people who are identical to us in every important way enjoy better technology: laser guns, intelligent robots, and spaceships that travel at the speed of light. Yet the revolutionary potential of future technologies is to change Homo sapiens itself, including our bodies and our minds, and not merely our vehicles and weapons. The most amazing thing about the future won't be the spaceships, but the beings flying them.

It's difficult for me to disconnect my own sense of identity from religion, though I am not someone who is 'religious' in the sense of following the dogma or tenets of a specific faith. Rather, like so many people in the world, I do believe in the interconnectedness of things and find a sense of wonder in the incredible truths that science brings in the explanation of everything. That said, however, I do often find myself, like so many people, wondering about the notion of God, and the spiritual.

How did religion and science emerge in society?

Justin Barrett: There are a number of different answers to this difficult question, and at this point we don't have compelling evidence to support one over another. The lens of your own theoretical orientation, and what evidence you are prepared to count, will also determine this. Some people assert the fact that we see evidence of symbolic behaviour around a hundred thousand years ago; for example, the Blombos Cave in South Africa.

Getting from symbolism to a belief in a higher power and the supernatural is a bit of a stretch. Material evidence suggests that a hundred thousand years ago, Homo sapiens were cognitively capable of the kind of thought that seems to be critical for religious thought. Whether or not they were engaged with it is something else. Fast-forward to around thirty to thirty-five thousand years ago, and we begin to see elaborate cave paintings and shamanistic depictions of humans and animals, which many people assert are in keeping with supernatural thinking. I'm sceptical. If we go back to twenty-five to fifty thousand years ago, we start to see very deliberate symbolic burials where people are being buried with goods and their bodies adorned. One could argue this suggests a belief in the afterlife. Maybe we're looking at the evidence wrong. Maybe we should be looking at when our ancestors seemed to have the right kind of conceptual capabilities that meant, when operating under normal conditions as we understand them today, it seemed to compel people towards religious thought.

What is the role of spirituality in our lives?

Sadhguru: The word spiritual has been hijacked by the religions of the world. Spiritual refers to the experiences in your life that have gone beyond the physical. Right now, everything you experience is happening to you only because you can see, hear, smell, taste and touch out of the sense organs. You cannot see or hear something that is not physical, you cannot taste, touch or smell something that is not physical. Your entire experience of the world right now is just physical in nature. You may say, 'What about thoughts and emotions?' They're physical too! They happen in your brain in the same way as digestion happens in your stomach. Whatever is physical within you right now is an accumulation from the planet. It's something you have gathered over time. When you were born, you were not the way you are right now. You slowly gathered your body. What you have gathered, you can claim as being yours, but you cannot claim it is you. So, what are you? The iPhone is now considered far more useful than the eye. For a whole lot of people, the smartest thing about them is their phone. If you have a phone, the more you know about it, the better you can use it, yes? So, if that's true of an iPhone, why do we not think of the eye in the same way? That's spirituality: to know this piece of life in its entirety from the origin to the ultimate end.

Bear Grylls: Well, for me, my Christian faith has been such a rock and backbone through so many ups and downs of life and adventuring. It is that real guiding force in my life that calms me, leading me home and strengthening me when I am tired.

I'm not altogether sure that science and religion are the antagonists that we sometimes think they are. Ultimately, they point towards the same basic human need to better understand who we are, and our place in the universe. The latter question has firmly become the domain of science in the past century, and the more we have come to understand the universe, the more we can be rapt with awe, not just with the almost unimaginable scales that we are dealing with when we think about space beyond our own solar system, but also at the unimaginably unlikely events that conspired to cause the Big Bang, and life in the universe. The most exciting and mind-bendingly complex area of study tackling these big questions in the twenty-first century is quantum mechanics, which examines life on an atomic and subatomic scale. It's the closest thing we have so far to a working model of how everything works. To understand more, I spoke with three of the world's foremost physicists and science communicators.

Can quantum mechanics help us understand the fundamentals of life?

Sean Carroll: We don't know a lot about the origin of life; we actually know more about quantum mechanics than we know about the origins of life! Life is this extremely complicated ongoing chemical reaction, and it needs to have started somewhere. Did it start automatically when the right conditions came together, or did it require some unlikely fluctuation to cause something unlikely to happen, which became robust and sustained itself? We don't yet know. It might be that life started as a very unlikely event that owed its existence to a quantum fluctuation; but we also know that life depends on chemistry, and chemistry depends on quantum mechanics. There are certain very, very specific features within biology that seem to rely on quantum mechanical phenomena in their own right. Photosynthesis is the most obvious one, our sense of smell might be another. Some people are saying that the connections between neurons in our brain also rely on quantum mechanics in some way. This is a frontier; this is something that we don't understand the details of. Life is hard enough to understand classically!

Does quantum mechanics have philosophical implications?

Jim Al-Khalili: The founding fathers of quantum mechanics were steeped in philosophy, and those different philosophical schools took quantum mechanics into different directions. In the history of science, we talk about it boiling down to an argument between Einstein and Bohr in opposing camps. Einstein believed there is a physical reality, an objective reality out there which physics was trying to explain. Niels Bohr was influenced by a school of thought called positivism, which said that if you can't agree a way of choosing a view you give up and go for a beer. It's pragmatic, instrumentalist. Essentially, Bohr said that the job of science and knowledge was epistemology, not ontology. The job of physics is not therefore to describe the world as it is, but to give us a way of saying what we can say about the world. Perhaps more than any other field in science, quantum mechanics has raised the question of what the job of science is. Is it reflecting what we can know but not touch? Or reflecting the world as it is?

Sean Carroll: There's a very good reason why many of the best and most influential scholars working in the foundations of quantum mechanics are people who have a PhD in physics but who are now employed as professors of philosophy. The type of thinking that a philosopher brings is well suited to the types of problems that quantum theory raises, and if you take quantum theory seriously, you're going to get a lot of philosophical questions – what those questions are, and what the implications are of those questions, will depend on your favoured version of quantum theory. Many-worlds theory, for example, doesn't just lead to different equations and quantitative predictions; it changes what we mean by personal identity. There is me, right now, here, but if I believe in many-worlds, at every instant, as the universe branches, there will be thousands of copies of me, thousands of copies of people who came from the same past self (me) but who are different, not the same as me. They are different people, living in different universes, but who share a common past identity. In the classical world, there is an idea that your personal identity stretches from the moment of your birth, to the moment of your death, in a unique line. Here's the thing: we have done experiments that show that what quantum mechanics says about the universe branching is absolutely happening. It's not that it can't be measured or understood, but rather that it requires a change in perspective.

Carlo Rovelli: They [the philosophical implications of quantum theory] are very vast. Quantum theory shows that the naive materialism of the seventeenth century mechanical philosophy is wrong. In other words, the real world is far different than material entities having definite properties at every time. I think what quantum theory really shows is that the properties of all entities are only defined at interactions and in relation to the other entities with which they interact. That is, reality is not a collection of objects with properties; it is a network of interactions and relative information. Life on earth is extraordinary in its diversity, yet the shared origins of that life are revealed through the science of genetics.

We now know that we share 98 per cent of our genes with chimpanzees, around 90 per cent with domestic cats and 85 per cent with mice. It's also interesting to note that we have a 60 per cent genetic similarity with bananas. As humbling as it is to understand our insignificance in our vast universe, it is also interesting in any discussion about who we are to consider the common ground we share with other species and living things on our planet when we contemplate our own existence.

Do other species experience consciousness like we do?

Carl Safina: Consciousness is simply the thing that feels like something. If you can feel or be aware of anything, that is consciousness! When you're given general anaesthesia and you're completely knocked out and not aware of anything, that's because you're unconscious. It strikes me as one of the symptoms of our chaotic confusion about the nature of the rest of the world and our relationship with the rest of the world that we don't understand and are continually confused over whether animals with eyes that can see, ears that can hear, noses that can smell and skin that can feel are 'conscious'. That's a very strange thing to still be asking. When I talk about consciousness, I mean that you're aware of things. Some people think consciousness means the ability to plan for the future, and things like that – that's not consciousness; it's something we learn to do, to the extent that we are capable of doing so.

How has your work with chimpanzees and great apes changed your view of humanity?

Jane Goodall: Louis Leakey wanted me to go and study chimps because he believed that 6 million years ago we had a human-like common ancestor. He was interested in Stone Age man, their skeletons, tools and so on – not behaviour. He felt that if there was similar behaviour exhibited between humans and chimps today, perhaps that behaviour would also have been present in the common ancestor and, arguably, in Stone Age men and women. From my perspective, it was a bit of a shock to find that chimps can be brutal and violent and even have a lot of warfare. I had expected them to be like us, but nicer. Because we have this tendency towards violence in certain situations, one can probably assume this trait [to be violent] has been with us in the long course of our evolution. Violence, at least some of it, is probably genetically based. You don't have to think much about humankind to realize that we are a very violent species. The difference between us and chimpanzees, with whom we share 98 per cent or more of our DNA, is not a sharp line. It's a blurry line. We are part of the continuum of evolution, and are not the only beings on the earth with personalities, minds, thoughts and feelings. We now realize how alike we are – kissing, embracing, holding hands, patting on the back, family bonds, war. But at the same time, we understand we are different. But what is it that's made us different? If you've got something that is as like us as chimps, you have somewhere to stand and observe the biggest differences. For me, our sophisticated way of communicating with words is that crucial difference.

Studies in anthropology tell us that art appeared before language – and that makes sense. We are a deeply expressive species, and we want to communicate not just through the written or spoken word, but through music, sculpture, painting and the many forms of art that culture has produced. There is something primal about our connection with art that helps us know things in a way that other forms of expression cannot. In my own life, I can attest to this. When I was going through a period of extreme depression, it was art, in particular poetry and photography, that helped me make sense of the world, and also to communicate what I was going through when I felt I couldn't. I explore art a lot more deeply in the next chapter, but I found from my conversations with some of the world's leading artists that the reason for the existence of art is as much to do with our expressions of self-identity as it is to do with connecting with others.

Why does art exist?

Antony Gormley: Art is the way that life expresses itself. It is something that all human beings do across all cultures and all continents. Creativity is intrinsic. When we tell a story in conversation, we are sharing an experience and offering it as a gift. This is the model. In telling and sharing, the experience is transformed. Visual art is not as intrinsic as singing, speaking or dancing, but is an extension and a concentration of the need to make sense of what happens to us. The need to express abstract registers of time and deep space, and something of the life of the body, has never altered. Art is not a luxury, an object of exchange, a profession or a career; it is an intrinsic part of being human. Art is an open space where hope and fear, future and past, come together; where the self – making sense of individual experience – becomes collective.

Marina Abramović: It's interesting to find the reason why cavemen had to make drawings in the middle of caves inside deep mountains. It looks like human beings, from the start of our existence, had to be expressive. The need to create is in our DNA. Hundreds of millions of people live without art, but I believe it's the oxygen of society. Good art has many layers of meaning. It can predict the future, it can ask the right questions (though it may not answer them), it can be disturbing, it can open your consciousness and really lift your spirits. Good art is a generator of energy; it's beautiful. People need to share this beauty with each other. Life can be so grey, and art gives it a touch of something else. If the artist is connected with divine energy, then the spiritual element can create immense power. For me as an artist, I see the public as an engine. I provide the key for the motor, but the audience become the work and functions without me. I create without even being aware of the consequences and possibilities. We are so lost right now – we have lost our spiritual centres. Just looking at art is not enough anymore; we have to be part of it.

Anish Kapoor: How can it be that we ever survived without art? As a species, we are afraid and fear is something one can perhaps push aside, but fundamentally it won't go away. Art is perhaps the means through which one shares fear, understands someone else's fear and knows a kind of fundamental humanity. Art is the means by which we understand the insignificance of being; what is a hundred years when seen in the context of hundreds of thousands, or even millions of years. In this way, art may be of even greater importance than life itself. Art can dare to ask questions such as, 'What is consciousness?' Science doesn't seem to get too far and offers a mechanistic explanation of this strange phenomenon. Art can speculate about this, and other fundamental questions, and give non-linear, poetic answers.

What is aesthetic beauty?

Philippe Starck: Nothing, nothing. Beauty, firstly, does not exist. It's just an opinion at 2.39 p.m. in London today, for example, and that's why I have no respect for this word 'beauty'. It is too volatile, which means it's nothing. You can change, whatever time you like, your opinion of what beauty is and what is beautiful. Today, this encourages vanity, cynicism, marketing, business, advertising, and everything like that. Beauty is definitively being turned into greed, to make business work, and to give some fake reason for people to buy more and more useless things. That's why I cannot accept beauty in its current form. For me, beauty is an obsolete word, from a time which was clearly bourgeois. I would, though, prefer to speak about coherence, harmony and balance of parameters. Sometimes you see a place, a painting, an action, a project, a child, a cat – anything at all – and you have a very strong structural feeling, which is very incredibly emotional. For me, I have had this feeling less than five times in my life, but in front of you sometimes, during one second or less, you can feel this emotion and say 'it is'. It's because the light was perfect, the temperature, the angle of view, your view, everything – all of the hundreds of parameters made this thing well balanced. Some people call that beauty – we can call it harmony.

※

Even if we live to the ripe old age of ninety, between a quarter and a third of that time will be spent in education. It makes sense; our world, our society, our economy and culture are all extraordinarily complex and to gain the cognitive apparatus we need to get by requires a lot of learning. It's also true that we spend the majority of our most formative years on this planet in some form of education and, perhaps inevitably, that education will have a profound impact on who we are when we grow up. I know my own world view and interests were inspired by my teachers at school, and it takes only a cursory read of autobiographies to realize how true this is for many others, too.

※

Why does humanity not access so much of its potential?

Deepak Chopra: Most people live under the hypnosis of social conditioning, meaning they do not question their everyday reality and rush to conform. Social conditioning is how we are educated, which in today's world is just an overload of information. Let's not forget the word education comes from the root *educare* – which means to nurture, support and bring out that which is already present in the mind. It should be the case that education brings out the potential for insight, creativity, wonder, curiosity and higher states of consciousness – things that are present in every single child that is born – but social conditioning camouflages and suppresses this, and pushes people to conform.

What is the role of education in society?

Ken Robinson: Education has four key roles in society, each of which is connected. Firstly, education serves an economic purpose, something which is often disputed. In the history of the philosophy of education, there have been many discourses and arguments about whether education should have any extrinsic purpose or whether it is an inherent good and should be done for its own sake. At every level, people do consider, however, that becoming educated will bring economic advantages to them personally, and that if their kids go to school and do well, they will be in a better economic position than they would have been otherwise. This is one of the reasons why governments invest so much money in education – they correctly assume that a well-educated population will be in a better position to contribute to economic prosperity. The big issue of course is to understand what kind of education we need to meet economic purposes these days. Secondly, education plays an important cultural role.

One of the reasons that we educate people – particularly our young people – is to initiate them into the cultural values, traditions and ways of thinking that characterize our communities. This is one of the reasons why there's such a heated contest over the content of a curriculum. Whenever people try to create divisive standards or curricula, it quickly becomes a very heated discussion. Thirdly, education plays an important social role. We expect education to play a role in helping students understand how their societies work and how they can play a part in them. Particularly within democratic societies, as John Dewey once said, 'Every generation has to rediscover democracy.' The fourth area is personal. Education should be about helping individuals discover their talents, their purpose in life, their sensibilities, their interests, and to enable them to live a life that's purposeful and fulfilling in its own right. In America just now, there's been a problem where kids have not been completing high school (I hesitate to use the word 'drop-out' as this implies they've failed the system, whereas, in fact, it's often the other way round – kids are just disengaging). As soon as we treat education as an impersonal process, a mechanistic and data-driven process, as soon as we lose sight of the fact that we're dealing with living, breathing human beings, then education ceases to be anything worthwhile.

⚙⚙

While the deep gaze of my cat may indicate that he is, indeed, having an existential crisis, it is highly likely that we humans are the only species on earth who are acutely aware of our own mortality, and that of all of our friends, loved ones and other species. It would be easy, therefore, for us to treat our lives as ultimately futile, but instead we expend an inordinate amount of our limited time on this earth in the noblest of pursuits: that of finding meaning. We are meaning-seeking animals and we need that something to help us make sense of life, who we are and why we're here. In the broadest sense, this is perhaps why we turn to art, religion and science as modes of enquiry to make sense of the world around us. In turn, we use the domains of the arts to better understand ourselves, and our place in the world. After all, identity is meaningless without a context.

Much of our language has been developed around the

linear, functional needs of society, but art is something else. As Anish Kapoor and Antony Gormley explained to me, art is a space where you can speculate, explore and generate non-linear answers. It's that hard-to-describe sense that we all have sometimes where a piece of art, music or even nature can spark a profound sense of understanding. This is a deeply intrinsic part of who we are – we are a storytelling species, and the earliest evidence of our species on this earth shows signs of that need to share our experiences as offerings, as gifts, to each other.

Our cognitive abilities have given the modern us a freedom beyond the immediacy with which the rest of the living world experiences life, but with that has come a sense of superiority beyond what we are. As Yuval Noah Harari says, this was not always so; it was only following the Agricultural Revolution that we began to see ourselves as essentially different from the rest of the animal kingdom – a strategy that once again manifested itself during the industrial era, as people were separated and classified by race to justify dominance and exploitation.

Like it or not, however, we are still animals. We have biases and characteristics that are part of our essential nature, which have been developed over tens of thousands of years, passed from generation to generation, optimized for a different world, one without the level of social interaction, technology and capability that we have today. It is because of this that we need to constantly learn and relearn what it means to be who we are. It also raises the question about who has the better deal: my cat, gazing out of the window waiting for the next bird to fly past, or me, gazing out of the window, wondering why life matters if all of us will die anyway. The best position is perhaps the middle ground – that we enjoy the experience of living physically, mentally, intellectually and culturally, while realizing that we are only temporary visitors to this beautiful world.

BIOGRAPHIES

Marina Abramović is a Serbian conceptual and performance artist, known for her work pushing the limits of the body. She is a member of the Royal Academy.

Professor Jim Al-Khalili is a theoretical physicist, best-selling author and broadcaster, and a University of Surrey Distinguished Chair, where he has also held a personal chair in physics since 2005 alongside a university chair in the Public Engagement in Science.

Professor Kwame Anthony Appiah is a British-Ghanaian author, cultural theorist and Professor of Philosophy and Law at NYU, and was awarded the National Humanities Medal at the White House in 2012.

Professor Justin Barrett is an American experimental psychologist and author, and Director of the Thrive Center for Human Development.

Professor Sean Carroll is a theoretical physicist and a research professor at the Walter Burke Institute for Theoretical Physics in the California Institute of Technology Department of Physics.

Professor Deepak Chopra is an Indian-born bestselling author and alternative medicine advocate. Founder of the Chopra Foundation, he is Clinical Professor of Family Medicine and Public Health at the University of California, San Diego.

Professor George Church is an American geneticist, molecular engineer, and chemist, widely known for his contributions in the sequencing of genomes. He has co-founded several companies and is a founding member of the Wyss Institute for Biologically Inspired Engineering.

Dame Jane Morris Goodall DBE is an English scientist and conservationist, considered to be the world's foremost expert on chimpanzees, and has received many honours for her humanitarian and environmental work.

Sir Antony Gormley is a renowned British sculptor and artist, creator of the *Angel of the North*, *Another Place*, *Field for the British Isles* (winner of the Turner Prize in 1994), *Quantum Cloud* and many others.

Bear Grylls OBE is a British former SAS serviceman, now a survival instructor, Chief Scout, bestselling author and television presenter.

Professor Yuval Noah Harari is a historian and philosopher, and the author of international bestsellers *Sapiens: A Brief History of Humankind*, *Homo Deus: A Brief History of Tomorrow*, and *21 Lessons for the 21st Century*.

Sir Anish Kapoor CBE is a leading British-Indian sculptor and member of the Royal Academy, who specializes in installation art and conceptual art.

Rose McGowan is an American actress, activist and *New York Times* bestselling author. She was named one of *Time* magazine's people of the year in 2017.

Sam Neill is an actor, writer, director and producer, best known for his starring role in *Jurassic Park*, and more recently in the hit TV show *Peaky Blinders*. He also owns his own winery near his home in Queenstown, New Zealand.

Dr Jordan B. Peterson is a clinical psychologist and Professor of Psychology at the University of Toronto, and author of multimillion-copy bestseller *12 Rules for Life: An Antidote to Chaos*, which has been translated into fifty languages.

Professor Steven Pinker is Professor of Psychology at Harvard University and internationally bestselling author of books including *The Language Instinct*, *How the Mind Works* and, most recently, *Enlightenment Now: The Case for Reason, Science, Humanism and Progress*.

Sir Ken Robinson (1950–2020) was a *New York Times* bestselling author, and an education and creativity expert. His TED talks have been viewed over 80 million times and his 'Do Schools Kill Creativity' presentation is the most watched TED talk of all time.

Professor Carlo Rovelli is a theoretical physicist and author of international bestsellers *Seven Brief Lessons on Physics*, *Reality is Not What it Seems* and *The Order of Time*, which have been translated into forty-one languages.

Sadhguru is an Indian yogi and author, and in 2017 was awarded the Padma Vibhushan, India's second-highest civilian award, for his contribution to the field of spirituality.

Dr Carl Safina is an ecologist, MacArthur Foundation 'Genius' grant-winning author and founding president of the Safina Center.

Dr Elif Shafak is a Turkish-British author, academic and women's rights activist. Her books have been translated into fifty-one languages and she has been awarded the *Chevalier de l'Ordre des Arts et des Lettres* in France for her contribution to arts and literature.

Philippe Starck is a French designer, architect and inventor. He is the powerhouse behind over 10,000 creations, including interior design, furniture, yachts and hotels.

Professor Jack Szostak is Professor of Genetics at Harvard University, and has been awarded several times for his contributions to genetics, including the Nobel Prize for Physiology or Medicine in 2009 (which he shared with Elizabeth Blackburn and Carol W. Greider).

ON CULTURE: THE CONTEXT OF HUMANITY

'There's something which impels us to show our inner souls. The more courageous we are, the more we succeed in explaining what we know.'

MAYA ANGELOU

It's impossible to remove humanity from culture; it is the context into which we are born and live our lives. In his 1658 painting *Blind Orion Searching for the Rising Sun*, Nicholas Poussin depicts the blind giant Orion being directed towards the healing rays of the sun by his servant Cedalion, who stood on his shoulders acting as his eyes. This metaphor explains well how culture comes to us. The generation of the living Cedalion is able to see further, by standing on the back of those who have gone before us – Orion. We inherit their now as our history, and build on it.

Culture is not a thing – it is everything. Every selfie, every tweet, every TikTok, every painting, every sculpture, song, novel, article, blog post, video. Everything we do as a society has a deliberateness, an aesthetic that goes beyond the function and allows that act to have a place in time and a purpose that we imbue. Our cultural artefacts are the components of telling the story of who we are.

John Berger, in his 1972 book *Ways of Seeing*, summed this up unsurprisingly beautifully: 'It is seeing which establishes our place in the surrounding world; we explain that world with words ... but words can never undo the fact that we are surrounded by it. The relation between what we see and what we know is never settled.' Being able to identify a 'thing' and understand the meaning of that same thing are also different and change over time. In the Middle Ages, for example, there was a belief in the physicality of hell that meant that fire became a real-world manifestation of that belief as an all-consuming, burning and painful phenomena – conversely, the concept of hell would also have carried significantly less significance had it not been for that physical embodiment. To put it another way, it was not enough to simply hold a sign up that says hell is bad. For us to get it, we needed the visual, the metaphor, such that we could temporarily accommodate the experience of hell into our being to make sense of it.

Growing up, my family used to visit India every year. Not just to see relatives, but usually to travel, often to far-flung remote parts of India where, as a child, I was thrust into a world very different from my suburban home in Manchester. Indian life is steeped in art and metaphor; things are not merely said with words, they are told with stories, pictures, dance, food and every tool at the creative disposal of the population. The intensity is deafening, like the surface of a stormy sea, until you are immersed into it, underwater, at which point everything makes perfect sense. It is perhaps because I experienced that profound cultural immersion at an early age that I spend a lot of my life seeking it out, whether that's through my own creative outlets (photography and poetry) or through consuming as much culture as I possibly can.

We are a storytelling species, and our shared stories are integral to our evolving collective identity. In this chapter are my conversations with some amazing novelists, including the great Maya Angelou, Elif Shafak and Yann Martel, who spoke to me about those stories that shape us. Of course, stories are told across so many forms, and to understand I have also included here some of my interviews with poets, including Lemn Sissay, George the Poet and Sir Andrew Motion; artist Tracey Emin; chef Heston Blumenthal; musicians including Black Thought, Moby, Lang Lang and Hans Zimmer; filmmakers Ken Loach and Paul Greengrass; as well as two of the most iconic photographers of the last century, David Bailey and Rankin. Their answers were fascinating to me, and paint a vivid picture of the most complex phenomena of humanity: our culture.

What is the role of storytelling in human culture?

Ed Catmull: Storytelling is our fundamental way of communicating with each other and informing each other. If we start from the beginning, one of the most rewarding things for the child and the adult is having the child on your lap while you tell them stories or read to them from a book. You are not only telling a story, but forging an emotional bond in doing that. Then, as a child, you go to school and receive another form of storytelling, where you're told the stories of our past, our history and our culture; what happened with our presidents, kings, revolutions and heroes. Whatever those stories are, they are always simplifications of what happened. We can never live through the events of the past – the only things we have left are the stories. The art form of storytelling is trying to figure out how you capture the essence, to inform someone about what's important in what happened, but they can never live it themselves.

Why do we write?

Maya Angelou: We write for the same reason that we walk, talk, climb mountains or swim the oceans: because we can. We have some impulse within us that makes us want to explain ourselves to other human beings. That's why we paint, that's why we dare to love someone – because we have the impulse to explain who we are. Not just how tall we are, or thin, but who we are internally, perhaps even spiritually. There's something which impels us to show our inner souls. The more courageous we are, the more we succeed in explaining what we know. When a poet writes a line that immediately translates from a black person to a white person, from an old person to young, or when a rich person writes a line that a poor person can comprehend, that's a success.

George the Poet: There's something magical in these sounds we call words. Words are loaded with meaning which is unique to the human experience. In all our hundreds of thousands of years of experience, we still don't know what a dog's bark means. Those sounds don't carry a specific relevance with us. We've been handed down language from generation to generation, and within it is coded so much human experience that when those sounds are organized deliberately with emotive effect? It's the closest thing we have to magic.

Yann Martel: I write because it passes the time in a creative way. I have the usual allotment of daylight hours, and between writing and pretty much anything else, I'd rather be writing. What's beautiful about writing is that it contradicts King Lear: something does come of nothing. Where once there was nothing, now there is a story and writing that story feels like the building of a cathedral. It's a slow, deliberate process. An initial idea leads to research; research leads to further ideas; ideas and research lead to copious notes; these notes become the structure of a story; then comes the writing and the rewriting until finally the story emerges, flowing as if it had been created spontaneously, with no premeditation. Creating that illusion, working on it, is deeply satisfying. As for why we write in this deep way, I think it's connected to our quest for meaning in life. Animals don't seek to understand why they are. We do. And stories – art in general – are the best way to find meaning, which, as an aside, is why religions, another meaning-creator, always tell stories.

What has been the role of the written word in social change?

Maya Angelou: It's interesting, but this made me think of an incident in the American Revolution. There was a patriot named Patrick Henry. The soldiers of the time were poorly fed, poorly dressed, poorly clothed, cold, wet and hungry. In order to keep their spirits up, Patrick Henry wrote inflammatory but beautifully eloquent lines. Since most of the soldiers were illiterate, he used to go up and down the rows of soldiers reciting these lines. One of them was: 'I know not what course others may take; but as for me, give me liberty, or give me death.' His words aroused order in the fighting men and, for a while, made them forget their misery. The written word, when it is really eloquent, when it doesn't have to be parsed or taken apart, when it speaks from one flame to another, speaks to a dying flame and reinvigorates. That's when it's powerful. That's true of all the passions, be they romantic, patriotic or otherwise. The written word confirms that you really can be more than you feel yourself to be right there, in that moment. When I was a young girl, I would read Shakespearian sonnets. At one point I thought Shakespeare was a black girl, a black American girl in the South. I had been sexually abused when I was young, and I stopped talking altogether from the time I was seven till the time I was about thirteen. At the time, I thought everyone could look at me and see that a man had abused me, and that they thought I had liked it. I read, 'When in disgrace with fortune and men's eyes, I all alone bemoan my outcast state,' and it connected with me – and then teachers told me that Shakespeare was a white man, an English man, that he lived four centuries earlier. I thought they couldn't possibly know what they were talking about. No white man could know what I feel.

Andrew Motion: Poems create change, but not in the same way that someone passing a law can. Poetry can't make you put on a seatbelt while you're driving! Poetry creates a world of possibilities and ambiguities, and allows us to see our world through a number of perspectives. If that is having the maximum effect on us, it will impact on how we behave in the world. Poems can also help us to crystallize ideas of the past. W. H. Auden once said, 'Poetry makes nothing happen,' and I know what he means. We might read that as a disappointment, but it might also be a relief! The rest of our world has this imbued intentionality – it's designed to make something happen. Auden writes about the 1930s as a low, dishonest decade. His writing profoundly affects our sense of what that time was like. If we face our present and future, and come to terms with it by understanding our past, Auden is actually a very good example of how the crystallization of a moment can change our future.

Lemn Sissay: Poems ride on horseback ahead of our journey. They are fierce chroniclers of the past and wild predictors of the future. They are statements of the present. If you want to know the voice of the people, listen to the poets and watch the artists. We learn more from the poets and the arts about the human condition than through any other medium. But poetry alone is dead. It must connect inside the poem, otherwise it is soulless, self-indulgent twaddle.

George the Poet: Poetry has no hiding places. You can't write poetry without making a stance. All you have is your words, and those words have to resonate. The most powerful will resonate universally. Human truths always prevail. If equality is true, if love is true, in the space of poetry it will come to the fore. You can't hide behind music, physical actions or anything else – you have to speak and be understood. The truth of poetry goes hand in hand with social change.

Black Thought: Art has always played a role in revolution, evolution and change. Art has always been a great changing force, the great common denominator, and a force to help people understand the world we live in and the people within that world. The darkest times in our history have brought about some of the most interesting art, in every genre. All the best forms of expression have come about during more trying and turbulent points in our story. Hard times are good for the arts – that's when people rise to their calling. When times are tough, that's when people look inside, find their purpose and speak to it. Art is a catalyst, a narrative, and is made up of the personal stories of the people who choose to be a part of its movement. Through art you can discover, at a very deep level, that there are other people in the world who feel the way you do, who see things the way you do, or want the change that you do. Art is our time capsule. It speaks to generations to come about what it was like to live in these days and times.

What is the role of storytelling in our culture?

Maya Angelou: We use it to encourage the new generation to understand something to allow them to step forward without going back, without having to repeat everything. That's the basis of folk tales such as Aesop's fables. The aim of storytelling is to get a message across, so the next generation can take it on without having to go back repeating my mistakes, or the mistakes I let myself make, or was fooled into making.

Yann Martel: It is the glue that binds us together. With no stories – personal, familial, local, national, global – we are nothing; that is, we're solitary animals, dumbly crossing a plain, not knowing where we are going or why. Stories define us, telling us who we are, giving us direction.

⚙☼

I didn't realize the power of poetry until I needed it. At school, poetry was something you had to study and dissect, like a frog; it never really meant anything to me, and I didn't understand it. But getting older, and experiencing the ecstasy of love, the pain of loss, as well as the depths of darkness, I realized that poetry has a power. It's not just words that rhyme – for me, it's like painting with words, and it somehow connects you deeply and directly to emotion and understanding like nothing else. Poetry became very personal for me as I went through a decade or more of serious depression. I was practically unable to communicate what I was going through until I found poetry gave me a voice. So, it's a part of culture that I hold extremely close to my heart.

What is the role of poetry in culture?

Maya Angelou: Poetry is written word, but it's also music, so it has a double strength. The written word, when in prose, has music within it, but it's not as heavily endowed with it. If you listen to poetry when it's spoken, you're drawn in. There's a magnetism that draws you to it and that's partly because of the music. People also don't stop to realize that the lyrics in The Beatles' songs, in blues and in spiritual music are all poetry. Young people say, 'I don't like poetry,' but they may love Elvis or Ray Charles, and they're all poetry.

Lemn Sissay: Poetry is at the heart of revolution and revolution is at the heart of the poet. What is the role of the poet in culture? I'm unsure if it's a question for a poet to answer. Although I have seen poets read for presidents and have read poetry in newspapers, I've seen poetry celebrate boxers and beauticians. I've seen poetry set to classical music and poetry in deep house music. I've seen poetry in punk rock and poetry in the charts. Poets nominated for the Mercury Prize and poetry at the National Theatre. Adele began as a poet. Amy Winehouse began as a poet. Don't think of me as someone desperately trying to find a link with an age-old tradition and the modern day. Just take a closer look and use your God-given eyes. Poetry is more popular now than it has ever been since the beginning of time. Big statement, right? But it's true. It is the poet's role to create. That is the only role in culture. I wish more people did it. I wish more people sat on the branch and cast their line into the vast open space of the imagination. The poet must express herself through the poem. This is how she proves herself to be alive. Cultural commentators of one sort or another will define the role of poetry and promote their definitions ad nauseam. The one consistent is the poet as creator of poem and this is all she need know. I wouldn't want to limit its role by defining it unless I'm coaxed down a rabbit hole. Sorry.

Saul Williams: The perceived distancing of poetry from the people is only true of some societies. If you go to Ireland, for example, poetry is very much alive – kids can recite Seamus Heaney. In the Middle East, kids can recite Rumi. Some cultures realize that poetry represents their essence. Poetry will always bring us back to our centre, and regardless of how far out we've gone in the spiral of business or capitalist mayhem, poetry always brings us home. Poetry operates in a safe space, but it's not always required to be safe. In many nations, poets are imprisoned! They can incite. They hold the keys to dismantle the system. They can make things clear, and can help our understanding of religion, humankind, society, gender and so many other topics. Poetry addresses the common stories of humanity in simple and complex forms, bringing light to these topics. When you identify poetry as culture, you are identifying the essence of culture. Something that isn't talked about in America much is the fact that when Alexander Graham Bell first created the phonograph (the record player), the first people he recorded were poets. Before radio, the most common pastime in America was to gather around the table after dinner and recite poems. The first recordings ever were poets. Just think about how important that is.

What makes a truly great piece of writing?

Maya Angelou: The truth. It either tells the truth, or it's not of very much use. If it tells the truth, whether it's Tolstoy writing it or Germaine Greer, Toni Morrison or Langston Hughes, or even Confucius, if it tells a real truth, a human truth, then the old white man who's sitting on his porch in Savannah, Georgia, or the Asian woman in San Francisco, or the rancher in Kansas, can all say, 'That's the truth.' Autobiography enchants me as a form. Years ago, I was asked by an editor in New York whether I would consider writing an autobiography. I said, 'No, I'm a dramatist and a poet,' and he said, 'Well, it's just as well you don't try. To make an autobiography, to write it really well, and to make it of importance, is almost impossible.' My close friend – like a brother – was James Baldwin. I know that editor said to James, 'Maya Angelou refuses to write, I don't know what to do,' and James said, 'If you want Maya to do something, tell her she can't do it.' Fifty years later, he still denies it.

Yann Martel: A great piece of writing contains a suitcase that can be opened at every age and affect us. So the *Iliad*, for example, despite being nearly three thousand years old, still moves us because of the situation the characters are caught in, the tragedy of their excessive emotions and the tragedy of the arbitrary pains that are sent their way by fickle gods. This suitcase can't just contain an emotive charge. That's essential, of course – if we feel nothing for a piece of writing, we will not involve ourselves with it. But the effect must go deeper. A great piece of writing must also illuminate intellectually. It must make one think differently. It's those two – emotive charge and intellectual insight – combined in a masterly fashion that allows a text to sail through time, ever fresh.

How does the written word sit alongside other forms of culture?

Maya Angelou: The written word is the base of culture, the spine. The other limbs and torso that attach to the spine, still depend upon the spine. Without the written word, there can be no other form of communication. One of the sadnesses I see today is young people who have no belief or faith in tomorrow. You see people who go from knowing nothing to believing nothing, and that's very sad. When people allow themselves no vocabulary with which to explain themselves to other people, and reduce their utterances to 'yeah', 'mmmhmm', 'I dig', it's very sad. You cannot, then, explain the delicacies of existence and the nuances of the human mind.

Yann Martel: We're verbal animals. Words are used in nearly every interaction between human beings. Not that silence and gestures don't have their place. But words are it. They make us human. So they find their way into nearly every human activity. Everything we do can be done to the song of words. We can speak as we make love, as we fight, as we dance. So there's no art form that I'm aware of that doesn't make use of words, at least in the conception. Visual arts and choreography, for example, may not use words in the final work, but words, spoken and written, will likely have been used earlier. So to answer your question: words sit alongside other forms of culture very well.

Can fiction and storytelling counter ingrained narratives around gender, sexuality, race, etc.?

Elif Shafak: Over the years, with each new novel I came to meet readers from diverse backgrounds. For instance, in Turkey, when you look at the people coming to my talks or waiting in the queue to have their books signed, you will notice how different they actually are. Among them are lots of leftists, liberals, secularists, feminists, but also Sufis and mystics. And then, conservatives and religious women with headscarves. Among them are Kurds, Turks, Armenians, Greeks, Jews, Alevis. To me this is incredibly important. In a country where everybody is divided into mental ghettos and isolated cultural islands, it matters to me that literature keeps its doors open to people of all backgrounds. I have to tell you, many of my readers in Turkey are xenophobic. This is the way they have been raised. So, if you ask their opinions about minorities, most probably they will say highly biased things. Likewise, many of my readers are homophobic. This is the only narrative they have heard in their society. But then the same people come and say to me, 'You know what? I have read your novel and this is the character that I loved the most,' and maybe the fictional character they are referring to is Armenian, Greek or Jewish, gay, bisexual or transsexual. I have thought about this dilemma a lot. How is it possible that people who are more biased and intolerant in the public space tend to become a bit more open-minded when they are alone? I don't think it is a coincidence.

What is the role of the written word in youth culture?

Maya Angelou: I don't mean to look down on Facebook and the like, but somehow, because we have technology – and because the television and other hangers-on have arrived – it seems things have changed. Texting has entered into the psyche so thoroughly that hundreds of people are being killed because they text while driving, and text while walking – and even walk into walls! It's really sad. I am not talking about throwing away technology. We have to build on our strengths and use what we have that has proven to be of use as fully as possible. Youth are not without their heroes and sheroes. Sometimes, especially when you hear the statements and utterances of their heroes and sheroes, you wonder why they chose them. I'm very blessed – I'm a six-foot-tall African-American woman, and when I go to the stadia, five thousand or ten thousand will pay to hear what I say. It's a blessing. Just now, a producer from another programme told me that I have over 3,800,000 fans on Facebook, and most of those people are young. That tells me people are asking for something, they want something. I try to tell them the truth, and hope it gets through. I'm not the only one; there are lots and lots of people who care enough about young people to try and tell them the truth, and encourage them to strengthen themselves.

Do you think writing must have an ethical or moral responsibility?

Maya Angelou: I think that's true for everybody – the butcher, the baker and the candlestick maker. Everyone has a moral responsibility to the other human being. You have to tell the truth in such a way that it can be seen and understood by another person, in another country. Like Terence said, 'I am a human being; nothing human can be alien to me.' When you look in the encyclopaedia, you see him – Publius Terentius Afer, known as Terence. He was an African slave, sold to a Roman senator, who was later freed by that senator. He became one of the most popular playwrights in Rome without ever knowing that he would become a citizen of Rome in that time. That statement and some of his plays stand here today, having come from 154 BC. 'I am a human being; nothing human can be alien to me.'

Yann Martel: No. Art is witness. It witnesses everything, the good and the bad. It's not just good people who write good books. And good books don't necessarily tell uplifting stories that have happy endings. Look at pop music. Pop lyrics are often quite depraved. Doesn't mean they're not great pop songs. But the truth is that writing is an effort and an artifice. It demands hard work. And it's rare the writer, I think, will go through all that work simply to negate life. I don't believe in literary nihilism. The true literary nihilist would simply not write. It's rather a starting point, a dilemma, which either the writer resolves to some extent, or the reader, applying his or her sense of irony.

Why does so much of our written culture reflect a nostalgic sense of past?

Elif Shafak: Well, I come from a society of collective amnesia. Walk around Istanbul and you will instantly notice what a rich history it has and yet our memory of the past is paper-thin. That contradiction has always struck me. I believe memory is a responsibility. Not to get stuck in the past but to learn from the past, to see its beauties and atrocities and complexities simultaneously. We need a nuanced and calmer approach to history. The problem with 'rational modernists' in the Middle East is that they are so future-oriented that they see their model as a total *tabula rasa* and they fail to notice the continuities in politics and society. The other extreme is shared by a wide spectrum of people ranging from populists to Islamists. These are people who are past-oriented. They sell a dream about a lost golden age. Why lost? Because they took it from us. Who is 'they'? The answer to this question varies as we move from one country to another. Foreigners or minorities or traitors or external powers. The rhetoric is deeply incendiary. This romanticized version of a glorious past is incredibly dangerous and toxic. I have been writing about how imperial nostalgia has resurfaced in the last decades in Russia, Austria, Hungary, Turkey, Germany. We need to pay special attention to those parts of Europe that were once upon a time multinational empires. This notion of 'lost grandeur' is constantly being exploited by populist demagogues in these places and beyond.

⚙⚙

The 'algia' in nostalgia can trace its roots back to the Greek *algos*, which relates to physical pain and distress. Research has shown that this bittersweet emotion is particularly prominent during times of change and uncertainty, and bittersweet is perhaps the best description – the sweetness of our ability to revisit and relive the good times, the bitterness of distance and even the realization of the impossibility of going back. Whether it's personal nostalgia (for our own past) or historical nostalgia (for a distant era), we romanticize and connect with nostalgic memories in a way that is deeply emotional – anyone who has experienced it will no doubt attest to this. The triggers for nostalgia are varied, but one of the most powerful is music – an art form, a language, that has the profound ability to revive memories with a level of lucidity that is difficult to attain from many other cultural forms.

What is the role of music in our experience of being human?

Moby: I think the human condition is just baffling for everybody. We are alive for a few decades in a universe that is 14 billion years old and vast beyond our imagining. We may define ourselves as having a fixed age of forty, for example, when the truth is that at a quantum level there is no part of you that is less than 14 billion years old. Music provides us with a strange self-generated celebration of the human condition in the face of a universe that is ancient and vast beyond our understanding.

Hans Zimmer: Music is one of the few things we, as humans, are any good at. If you look at the history of music, way back, you will find things like the Balinese monkey chants. It starts out as a bunch of monkeys yammering in a forest and turns into a chant. If you go to any rave, or any football event, you will find people chanting in a rhythm – human beings do that. We have this sense to participate and organize. This is music at its most crude form. We then go to something more sublime like the second movement of the Mozart Clarinet Concerto; you can't fail to be moved by it! Music lets you rediscover your humanity, and your connection to humanity. When you listen to Mozart with other people, you feel that somehow we're all in this together. This is, I suppose, what great poetry strives for.

What is the art of performance for you?

Lang Lang: For me, there is no distance between the performer and the instrument, which with a piano is not easy. With a guitar, you pick it up and hold it – it's like having a friend next to you. With a violin; it's like playing music *with* the instrument. A piano has this physicality to it; it's standing there and you have to put more effort in to get the instrument to play. You can't sit there and let your hands play; you have to get connected through your head and your heart before you even play one note.

Is genre an extension of culture?

Moby: All the variables that contribute to the birth, sustenance and morphing of a genre, and the way in which people feel married to a genre, enter the realm of chaos theory. The variables are myriad and unknowable. You could give a glib answer and say that rock 'n' roll came from white trash guys who liked black R&B – but it's so much more complicated than that. I don't want to sound too esoteric, but I do think a lot of this has to do with neural plasticity. As time passes, neuroscientists become more aware of how fluid and plastic the brain can be, but research also shows there is a wilful desire to hold on to a degree of rigidity – maintaining things that are familiar, and to which we have allegiance. We see this a lot with patriotism and attachment to sports teams, but it also leads to genre. It's not just a preference, but an atavistic tribal allegiance. There used to be a utilitarian aspect to this. When records were expensive and hard to come by, the purchase of one used to be an expression of allegiance to a genre. Now, music is ubiquitous and barely costs anything, so it seems that as time passes, genre is becoming more of an antiquated idea. If we were having this conversation thirty years ago, almost everybody you and I were friends with would have had genres they were very deeply attached to. When I think of all of my friends now, rarely do they speak in terms of genre, but rather in terms of music that they like.

Hans Zimmer: Absolutely! For example, I have always believed that rap music, in one way or another, grew out of the blues and work songs. It's a genre where pretty strong political and social ideas are expressed. European art music, on the other hand, comes out of a need to play nice music for people's expensive dinner, or the opera. One is real and authentic and charges forward, while the other is becoming redundant and hanging on for dear life. You have so many varieties. Militaristic music, which I don't think is music at all – in fact I believe it is a horrible proclamation, a misuse of music. There's a reason why there are a million and one love songs – they all try and say the same thing, albeit in slightly different ways. In popular music, you have the notion of the band. There is something about being young and coming together with three other guys to form a band and make music. It's a natural thing. To make great music, you have to have that certain recklessness which you have when you're young. I think this is why a lot of bands fall apart. The recklessness and the adventurousness is there, but I don't think they know how to be socially fair to each other. They have to behave as one single body, with collective responsibility for the sound they make.

Lang Lang: When you speak of classical music, you are really speaking of a period, not a genre. Within that umbrella you have baroque, romantic, impressionist, contemporary and many more genres of classical. Many people have the wrong understanding and hear something and think, 'Ah, this is classical,' when, in fact, it is just like any other music but perhaps more structured, more calculated. Music is there to express personal moments, emotions and passions. That may be through a three- or four-minute pop song, a thirty-minute sonata. They will both take you on an emotional journey, just with different peaks and valleys. Regardless of genre, the idea of making music is the same; it's there to express your personal opinions.

What is the relationship of music to language?

Moby: This is an issue that Western philosophy has been dealing with for millennia: the question of what can be known and how it can be communicated. In the early twentieth century when Ludwig Wittgenstein wrote the *Tractatus Logico-Philosophicus*, he basically tried to answer this question, saying that the only meaningful way that human beings can communicate is through mathematics. He felt this [maths] was a language that left no room for interpretation or subjectivity. A few decades later, he almost refuted this. He didn't say that art, speaking and writing had no meaning, but rather that they were inherently subjective forms of communication. Music transcends the limits of language. The English lexicon is vast, but still is limited. Music comes in to fill the gap. It looks at the way we can't express ourselves through the spoken or written word and makes up for the lack.

Hans Zimmer: Music is definitely an extension of language. Bernstein explained this beautifully in his Harvard Lectures where he talked on how music came about. We have one universal word, 'mama'. If you sing it a little faster and a little louder, mama will hear you and come and feed you. In this sense, music had a survival necessity. Like all good things, sooner or later we get past bare survival and turn things into art.

Lang Lang: Music stays with you. If you keep practising and keep playing, it will be with you for your whole life – and what a gift that is. In my own life, the fame and other things are obviously important, but *nothing* can replace the gift of music in my life. It's the real treasure I have. The gift of music is like the treasure you find on a treasure island. You don't have to be a master; it's an art that can give you a fantastic feeling, regardless of your skills, age, wealth, location. It will stay with you – it's special, unique, beautiful. Successful music stays in our hearts. It may be Bach or Beethoven; it may be K-pop or EDM. It's like the great works of Shakespeare – the pieces that connect with our hearts hold a really unique position in society, like traditional fairy tales, novels or plays. Music remains in our roots, and helps us grow, improve and be better. It reminds us of our past, and also speaks to our present day and our future.

⚙⚙

There may appear to be a disagreement between Moby and Hans here, but whether we consider music to be an extension of or transcendence from language, the thesis is broadly similar: that music allows communication of concepts that cannot be adequately conveyed in our traditional written forms.

For me, it's impossible to tell the story of culture without film. The moving image has been with us as long as we have made art. From prehistoric shadowgraphy, through to shadow puppetry and camera obscura, we have been fascinated by creating and observing moving depictions of culturally and socially significant aspects of life. It was not until the mid-1800s, as technology became sufficiently advanced, that we began to see film, as we would recognize it today, being produced – inventors and artists started not just to document life, but to create narratives to tell stories. There is something primal and comforting about how we connect to moving images; perhaps because we are hardwired to detect and respond to motion in our environment. That direct connection from moving image to emotional response may explain why film and cinema dominate culture.

⚙⚙

Why has film become such an important part of culture?

Paul Greengrass: Films are commerce and art; that's been the way since the beginning, like theatre. Film has a central place in culture because it's demotic, everyone can access and understand it – moving pictures have an instant accessibility, they get into your unconscious mind. There is a beauty to the collective experience of going to the cinema. The great David Lean used to say that when he was a boy, and went to the cinema, he looked at the beam of light coming down towards the screen as if it were the light coming through a cathedral window; it gave him a pious sensation – and there's something to that. Cinema has a mystery, a magic. That's not to say it's better or worse than any other art form, but it has an emotional potency as a creator of moods and memory. It has the power to make people jump, make people move, make people cry, make people identify with characters who are like them or who they would like to be.

What is the role of cinema as a mode of expression?

Ken Loach: Cinema has always been this contradiction. On one hand, it's a medium that provides almost infinite possibilities in terms of images, sound, drama and observation. It uses stories like novels and theatre, uses sound, music, and has all these elements which can then be edited to do anything. The possibilities of cinema are wide and deep, so why shouldn't it use that language expressively? Well, cinema has always been a commercial undertaking too. From the first shows, they were like diversions – connected to fairs, commerce and entertainment. Right at the onset of theatre you had the Elizabethan, Jacobean dramatists who were writing as profoundly as anyone as could imagine, but in cinema, you didn't have that. It was commerce. These are the two tensions. Commerce is in the hands of multinational companies, cinemas are owned by multinational companies – and cinema is just one part of a range of interests of these huge companies. The financial pulling power can be seen in the form of Hollywood or Bollywood – money has ruled what cinema has become and the rest of the industry is left with a tiny fragment of space, better known as art houses. Even they are now becoming owned by multinational companies, and so films that do not have a big commercial element have a narrow chance of success. A lot of people want to make creative, expressive cinema – but there just isn't the space left to show it.

What constitutes a great story?

Ken Loach: I've always worked directly with writers, and stories often come out of those conversations – and shared views of the world. A good story reveals a whole truth about society – it's not just a group of characters. You have to reveal something more profound than just those individual lives or situations; a story is a conversation. You will get a hunch of what is significant, what's cutting, what's imaginative, what's funny. The aim for me is to find a story that may seem small, but which sheds light on a much deeper issue or conflict; a microcosm that reflects something much greater.

⚙️⚙️

Cinema is undeniably powerful and in India you see this viscerally. Film for most Indians has become almost inseparable from identity. The more than a thousand films released each year in Bollywood (the catch-all term for Indian cinema) are the forum through which billions of Indians reflect on issues of society and culture. Stars of the screen are worshipped in a manner close to idolatry, and carry incredible power and influence in India. Growing up in an Indian diaspora household I saw this first-hand. For my parents, not only was Indian cinema a nostalgic link back to 'home', but it was also a way of understanding the ebb and flow of the transformation of Indian culture through time.

What is the relationship of film to Indian culture?

Siddharth Roy Kapur: Indian cinema has been in existence for more than a hundred years, and for most of that time it has been really the primary mode of mass entertainment for our country. India has, for a long time, been a very poor country and it's only in the past decade and a half that we've been able to pull a fair number of people above the poverty line; but we have a long way to go. In an environment like that, cinema formed a means of escapism for people, from what they had to go through in their daily lives. Those three hours in a movie theatre gave people a chance to forget their woes and become one with their hero or heroine on screen. That is also perhaps why so much of our cinema has been escapist entertainment – people's lives were hard enough without them having to deal with those same harsh realities on screen. Cinema is integral to Indian culture, has deep roots in daily life, and regardless of the platform, has just as much resonance today as at any time before.

Is Indian cinema reflecting a more diverse nation?

Ritesh Sidhwani: When we were shooting *Made in Heaven*, Section 377 of the Indian Penal Code had ruled that consensual same-sex acts were unconstitutional and thus illegal. In this series, we had depicted same-sex relationships, and expressing these things would have been a serious infringement of the law! In a secular, democratic country, where liberal values were growing, this went against what we stood for. By the time we had finished shooting, the Supreme Court had abolished Section 377, and it meant a lot of people could express their freedom and talk about it. Sometimes, you do get a certain idea and get inspired because it's important for that story to be told. Sometimes you hear this groundswell across the country around an issue, and that creates narratives that need to be shared and expressed. Indian audiences are exposed to culture from around the world, and even content from elsewhere can inspire and influence culture, and the stories told to and of culture.

Siddharth Roy Kapur: Even in the 1940s, 50s and 70s we had plenty of films that spoke to the taboos of society, but today we're seeing a much greater diversity of subjects in Indian cinema than we've had before. Traditionally, Indian cinema has had to be all things to all people; films had to have a mix of romance, tragedy, comedy, great songs, dances, an imposing villain, gorgeous stars and great locations. For a film to be successful, it had to have all of that – and that's the Bollywood genre, right? As tastes have widened, and we're exposed to more global cinema, people have moved to a level where they're ready to be able to enjoy something that is not just escapism. You are dealing with subjects that talk to society as it is today, and while the escapist fare still does extremely well, you now have a whole other array of commercial cinema that deals with subjects which, just a few years ago, would have been relegated to art-house cinema or parallel cinema.

What is the role of music in Bollywood?

Ritesh Sidhwani: Everything in India is celebrated with music! A wedding would not be complete without a sangeet evening. Music is ingrained, we express everything with music. In cinema, whatever the situation, whether it's celebrating, mourning, grieving, it's brought to life with music. It is as much a part of our culture as, say, martial arts are to Chinese culture. In earlier times, however, you'd suddenly have characters that break out into song and you'd have these dream sequences where suddenly your characters are on the Swiss Alps, romancing around a tree. But that's changing, and music is now being seamlessly written into screenplays. Of course, there are exceptions. In our film *Gully Boy*, we had eighteen or nineteen different tracks made in collaboration with over thirty artists. Everything in that film was expressed through music, specifically the underground rap circuit, which was not considered mainstream in India, but which was the hook for the film – it was a powerful subculture which deserved to become mainstream.

Siddharth Roy Kapur: Indian movies have always used music in their narratives extremely effectively and extensively. While the way it's used may change (we don't have that many playback songs any more with lip-sync), we still have those musical underlays to movie sequences that bring out the stories and help the writer to tell the story they want to on screen.

{gears}

As an art form, photography is able to communicate something unique; it is a fixed moment in space and time that tells a story, much like the written word. This connection between writing and the image is perhaps why it is no accident that the word photography itself is derived from the Greek words *phos* (for light) and *grapho* (for writing) – but photography has a much deeper cultural meaning for us, as writer and philosopher Vilém Flusser explains: 'Images are mediations between the world and human beings. Human beings "ex-ist", i.e. the world is not immediately accessible to them and therefore images are needed to make it comprehensible.'

{gears}

What is the role of photography in culture?

David Bailey: Photography was the first great recording, allowing people to record the moment. The moment is the only thing you've got when you think about it. As we're talking now, we're already history, but a photograph can turn it into a moment. Forget all the art shit and all that nonsense – people keep albums to keep memories alive. Your brain can't cope with all your memories. As you get older, your hard drive gets overloaded. If you see a snap from the 1970s or whatever, you might think, 'Oh, I remember that moment!', but if you didn't have it, the moment would have been gone for ever, and nobody would remember it. Photography is a great moment-taker, much more than movies.

What is the role of photography in understanding ourselves?

Rankin: That's pretty complex as I know a lot of people would probably say that photography actually confuses us more than it helps us understand ourselves or the world. To me, photography is a tool and like most tools it can be used for good or bad. When you pick up a camera, I think you have a responsibility that goes with that camera; what are you going to use it for? At its best, I think the best photographs in any genre – documentary, fashion, art – attempt to hold a mirror up to society, try to show it for what it is, to expose or bring attention to, say, how ridiculous or incredible it is. At its worst, photography can be used for pure evil and at its most banal it gets used to sell stuff. I see the selfie as an attempt to use photography to sell a false ideal of yourself to yourself. How sad is that!

Can photographs change the world?

David Bailey: A photograph stopped the Vietnam War, I think – the girl on fire. It's just a press picture. That's not art, it's being there. Taking a picture and making a picture are two different things. I'm not saying taking a picture isn't important – it is, if it's the right picture, in the right place. But you can't call it art – if there were five hundred photographers stood next to you, they would all have taken the same fucking picture. The other famous picture, of the bloke shooting a guy? Turns out it gave the wrong impression because the bloke was a real arsehole.

I then asked David about today's world: what does photography teach us about the world we live in?

There are too many people in the world. Politicians go on about petrol, but the simple thing, which is so obvious, is that there's too many people. Eventually, the world won't be able to take it. Scientists aren't going to solve it, unless we can find a cheap way to go to other planets; and they're not going to do that. It's a bit like Easter Island – they cut down all the trees, burnt them and they were stuck on the island. And the earth is just an island in the universe. The only other thing that could unite the human race is the discovery of aliens.

I also asked him what he thought about aliens, about those unknown phenomena – and about God.

I can only go by my common sense, which is very limited. If I met God, I wouldn't be able to comprehend him anyway. I don't believe in God. I believe there's something else, maybe quantum maths, who knows? Or maybe we're the dream of Krishna, who knows? Collective electricity – I don't know what the fuck it is, and if someone showed me, I couldn't comprehend it; my brain's not big enough. We'll never find out who God is, our brains just aren't big enough! There's a story that when Captain Cook first came into contact with Aborigines, they couldn't see his boats because they couldn't comprehend them. That's a bit like seeing God, on a lower level.

Rankin: I'm a great admirer of Toscani, who, for me, made some of the boldest statements you'll ever see in advertising. He went so far the other way with his approach that it made people stop and think about what they were doing in life.

His Colors of Benetton campaigns were so in-your-face yet extremely simple, which is why they were so shocking. I think they are a good example of how images that might be from what is normally seen as an insipid genre can change the way people think. As a photographer it's so important to remember the person, the human being that we all are. Whether it's somebody in the Congo or an A-list celebrity, it only takes one image to change societies' opinions or the general consciousness. As I've said, for me, the best imagery is about exposing something to the world that the world's never seen before, or putting a mirror up to society and being critical or ironic, amusing or celebrating it.

What is the power of art?

Tracey Emin: This is going to sound really nutty, but just go along with me on this. I can't prove it, but I really, really, really do think that true art – art with conviction, with emotion – carries a certain amount of weight, like the weight of things, the emotional weight of the world. It's like all that emotional hell, screaming, passion and whatever else goes into the artwork is sucked into it, and they just emit, like capsules, pulsing and breathing wherever they exist. Art takes the strain, takes the pressure, takes the fear, takes the indulgence. It's like an atom of sorts, all this emotion that has gone into these paintings, into these atoms of paint, glued together. They don't explode, they don't go crazy, they just live on a wall shaking. That's why art needs to exist. That's also how I know when my own work is good and when it isn't, and it's why I paint over such a lot of what I do. I can paint a good picture – fucking hell, it's so easy for me to do that – but it's not about that. That's the job of a picture maker, and I'm not a picture maker. Art is about something else for me. If I don't do it how I want to do it, there's no point.

What is the relationship of younger generations to art as a movement?

Black Thought: I don't think the art, the fashion, the sound of millennials is catered to the palate of someone my age, but nevertheless it's art. It's their art. The medium of the art of millennials is technology and that's how they express themselves. It's not necessary or intended for us to understand. I try to appreciate it for what it is. It may seem shallow at face value, but it has its own truth and depth. There are many millennials who make visceral material. If I think back to when I was in my twenties, I wasn't necessarily as concerned with what people my parents' age thought about what I was doing as I was about what my peers felt.

⚙⚙

An examination of culture, however, would be incomplete without considering food. Food is not just one of the basic things needed by all living things for survival (alongside air, water, shelter and habitat); it is nutrition, nature, culture, spirituality, social good, desideratum, an aesthetic object and art. It is simultaneously the most social and intimate of activities, engaging our senses in a manner rarely achieved by any other aspect of our lives. Most of our global cultures are defined by their relationship with food; it is a way of communicating identity and heritage, as well as being deeply symbolic and playing a central role in many ceremonies. Growing up in a Hindu household, there was little doubt for me about the cultural importance of food; it was everything. Heston Blumenthal and Alain Ducasse are two of the most important chefs of our generation, but much more than that, they are philosophers and renaissance thinkers. To better understand the role of food in culture, I could not think of a more perfect pair to speak to.

$$\{\circ\}\{\circ\}$$

Why is food so important to us?

Heston Blumenthal: We have the unique ability to imagine things that don't exist, enabling us to create shared beliefs and culture: language, religion, science, maths, music, farming, dancing, social media, states, nations, football teams – these are all shared beliefs. And of course, you have the two biggest shared beliefs: money and time. Behind all this is consciousness, the evolution of which is closely linked to our ability to find food – and today, we don't have to climb mountains and kill to feed our family. Food has become easy to get. We've domesticated ourselves! Our most intimate relationship is with air – we need it to breathe – and then the liquids and solids we put in our mouth for fuel. After that, it's with other objects and creatures – mountains, fish, animals, everything. First, in order to have a journey at all, though, you need to drink and eat.

As a species, we began as hunter-gatherers, where small groups of people would keep each other alive by finding food. Our entire endocrine and hormonal system was developed through this process. We had to develop shared culture around food to survive. We hunted and gathered, prepared and ate, and were driven by hormones and emotions. Imagine those early humans finding a mushroom on the forest floor. In that group, someone had to be the first to take a bite of that mushroom and, if they survived, they could tell others, 'That one's fine, we can eat that.' And that's how it was for thousands of years, keeping each other alive through food. Fast-forward a few thousand years, and we had the emergence of agriculture; we cultivated and grew, and we had a surplus to trade – we went from valuing the moment as hunter-gathers to valuing the asset of food and being fearful of losing it. Fast-forward a few thousand more years to today: we live in a society where most common diseases are almost eradicated, replaced with diseases like loneliness, diabetes, Alzheimer's, dementia, Parkinson's and so on – but we generally live longer and, relatively, more comfortably than ever before, and so we're fearful of losing that.

What is the role of food in our culture?

Heston Blumenthal: 13.8 billion years ago, a big bang happened. Not *the* Big Bang, but a big bang. As a result of that interaction, molecules and atoms formed (chemistry), some of those formed organisms (biology), all of them exist in a system governed by mathematics and predictable structures (physics) and some of those organisms evolved consciousness (history). Cooking and eating are the only way you cross all of these areas. You get plants, meat, fish, fruit, ingredients, and you do something to them. You chop them, heat them, put them in coal – you do something to them (physics). That produces physical and chemical reactions that produce aromas and textures as the molecules and particles change (chemistry). You eat it (that's biology). If you like it, maybe you'll write a recipe (history). Food covers everything: physics, chemistry, biology, language, mathematics, music, dance, philosophy, psychology, geology, geography – everything. Yet we've taken it off most of our curricula and don't give it the educational attention it deserves. The responsibility is not for me, or you, as individuals, but to make sure that we teach kids about food – and how that can give them the opportunity to be more aware of themselves, their connection to the world, and each other. The more you relate to the food you eat, the more you are consciously present as you eat – the less you eat, because you value the food more. It's mindfulness. You can dig your hand into a bowl of raisins and stuff your mouth, or you can take each raisin, look at its structure, texture, feel it, and then really examine the taste as you eat it, the flavour, the sensation, your relationship with it. It's intimate, and we take it for granted.

Alain Ducasse: Food is central to human lives – whatever the epoch, wherever in the world. Brillat-Savarin said it very rightly: 'Tell me what you eat, I'll tell you who you are.' First of all, food is a link between humans and nature. Eating requires selecting produce considered as eatable. It also encapsulates a cultural vision of what a meal must be: what to eat according to circumstances, how to prepare the dishes and, most importantly, how to share this moment. The table is a concentrate of humankind. It is the most civilized place in the world.

I don't wish to downplay the challenges of your life, or mine, but in comparison to the horror of existence for the vast majority of the story of our species, we have it, for the most part, relatively easy. For most of our time on this planet, our life expectancy was frighteningly short – close to a third of what we now consider relatively normal – and most of that life was a fight for sheer survival, perhaps closer to what we now consider life in the natural world.

Our superpower, however, comes in the form of a squishy 1.7-kg supercomputer that we all carry around with us – a device that not only gives us a sense of consciousness, but also allows us to position ourselves in space and time. Thus we, as individuals and groups, know we have a history, a future and a mortality, and this is reflected in our culture. As Yann Martel told me, as far as we know, animals don't seek to understand who they are, but we do. Maya Angelou echoed this sentiment when she described how we all have an impulse within us that makes us want to explain ourselves to other human beings through art, through love, through the written word. It sets us apart from other species, and is perhaps our greatest gift.

Art is a meaning-finding pursuit, and alongside the earliest fragments of human presence, we find evidence of this as our glyphs and depictions share knowledge, news, beauty and even the basal assertions of existence – the historic equivalent of scrawling 'I woz 'ere' into stone. As we advanced, so too did the assertions of our existence and the ways in which we shared knowledge and history. We developed more sophisticated language, art, poetry, music and film – more sophisticated ways to assert our existence, to share our stories, our knowledge, our history and our future. Art as culture has always been a great changing force, the great common denominator, to help people understand the world we live in, as well as each other.

Culture is the amalgamation of this; it gives context to our lives, and a lens for us to make sense of everything. As Yann Martel said during my interview with him, without culture, without stories, 'we're simply solitary animals, dumbly crossing a plain, not knowing where we're going or why'. Stories in the form of culture give us the answer; they tell us who we are, and the trajectory of where we travel. Culture is abstract, yet tangible – and if we were to be poetic and ask what culture is made of, I think the answer would be simple: our truth.

BIOGRAPHIES

Dr Maya Angelou (1928–2014) was an American poet, memoirist and civil rights activist. She is best known for her series of seven autobiographies, which began with *I Know Why the Caged Bird Sings*.

David Bailey CBE is a fashion and portrait photographer who is credited with helping create the 'Swinging London' of the 1960s and was the inspiration for the lead character in the film *Blow-Up* (1966).

Black Thought is an American rapper and the lead MC of the Grammy award-winning hip-hop group the Roots, which he co-founded with drummer Questlove.

Heston Blumenthal OBE is a British celebrity chef and TV presenter. His restaurant, The Fat Duck, one of five restaurants in the UK to have three Michelin stars, was voted number-one restaurant in the world in 2005.

Ed Catmull is an American computer scientist, co-founder of Pixar and president of Walt Disney Animation Studios.

Alain Ducasse is a French chef and is the owner of over twenty restaurants around the globe, including three with three Michelin stars.

Tracey Emin CBE is an artist and member of the Royal Academy of Arts. She is known for the autobiographical nature of her work, which she produces in a variety of media, including drawing, sculpture, film and neon text installations.

George the Poet is a British spoken-word artist, poet, rapper and award-winning podcast host.

Paul Greengrass is an award-winning film director, producer and screenwriter. He is widely known for his use of handheld cameras and dramatizations of historic events.

Siddharth Roy Kapur is a film producer, founder and MD of Roy Kapur Films, and President of Film and Television Producers Guild of India. He was previously Managing Director of The Walt Disney Company India.

Lang Lang is a Chinese concert pianist, educator and philanthropist. He has performed with renowned orchestras all over the world.

Ken Loach is a filmmaker renowned for his socially critical directing style and socialist ideals. His film *Kes* was voted the seventh greatest British film of the twentieth century in a BFI poll and he has twice won the Palme D'Or at the Cannes Film Festival.

Yann Martel is a Spanish-born Canadian author of the Man Booker prizewinning *Life of Pi*, which has sold 12 million copies worldwide and was made into an Academy award-winning film.

Moby is a musician and producer who has sold 20 million records worldwide. Outside of music, he is known for his animal rights activism.

Sir Andrew Motion is an English poet, author and biographer. He was Poet Laureate of the United Kingdom from 1999 to 2009 and is the founder of the Poetry Archive.

Rankin is a portrait and fashion photographer, and director. He is the co-founder of *Dazed and Confused* magazine, founder of *Hunger* magazine and Rankin Film. He has shot portraits of many celebrities, including Kate Moss, David Bowie and Queen Elizabeth II.

Dr Elif Shafak is a Turkish-British author, academic and women's rights activist. Her books have been translated into fifty-one languages and she has been awarded the *Chevalier de l'Ordre des Arts et des Lettres* in France for her contribution to arts and literature.

Ritesh Sidhwani is an Indian film producer and executive, and co-founder of Excel Entertainment with Farhan Akhtar.

Lemn Sissay MBE is a poet, bestselling author of *My Name is Why*, and was awarded the PEN Pinter Prize in 2019. He was the official poet of the Olympic Games in 2012 and is Chancellor of the University of Manchester.

Saul Williams is an American rapper and musician specializing in a blend of poetry and hip hop. He also has a career as an actor and starred in the 1998 independent film *Slam* and the 2013 musical *Holler If Ya Hear Me*.

Hans Zimmer is a German film-score composer and record producer who has composed music for over 150 films, including *The Lion King*, for which he won the Academy Award for Best Original Score in 1995.

3 ON LEADERSHIP: BRINGING HUMANITY TOGETHER

'Leadership is the need to change things for the better, and that starts with people. It's about figuring out how to get a group of people, in particular circumstances, to keep moving forward.'

JOHN KOTTER

Let me be perfectly clear; if indeed there is such a thing as a born leader, it's definitely not me. I was a shy, unpopular kid – I didn't play team sports, never led a school activity and came from quite a reserved household and culture. If you had asked one of my teachers to pick the natural leader from the thirty or so kids in my class, I would have been number twenty-nine or thirty. When I started my first 'business', the aim was not to be a business leader, but rather to make enough money to pay for flying lessons, so I could follow my dream of becoming an airline pilot. What I didn't recognize at the time was the passion that would emerge for running a business, for the cut and thrust of negotiating, for delivering products and services to our customers, and for working with brilliant people who I could bring into the business to help it grow. I had to learn to lead 'on the job'. I realized very quickly that the key was to bring my team with me on our mission to be the best web design agency in Europe, and to deliver the smartest software solutions for our clients.

I didn't have the business parlance for it at the time, but I was creating what would be more accurately described as a high-performance culture that allowed people to grow and flourish. I had to quickly understand what I was good at (strategy) and not so good at (keeping the trains running on time), and I came to realize that it was perhaps an advantage that I had always been the shy kid – confidence is important, but too much can be dangerous. In my view, there is no endgame with leadership; you learn every single day, and from every single crisis (and we've had a few!).

My experience of leadership has been firmly in the world of small and medium enterprise with organizations responsible for staff in the hundreds. While I have been on the board of several entities with many thousands of employees, they have not been my direct responsibility. It is with this in mind that I have always been fascinated by the art and science of great leadership – what it takes to lead some of the largest organizations in the world, and what we as leadership minnows can learn from those at the very top.

In this chapter, we will meet some of the world's most successful and impactful leaders. Starting with perhaps the most profound area of leadership, the armed forces, I talked to General Stanley McChrystal (former Commander of Joint Special Operations), General Richard Myers (former Chairman of the Joint Chiefs of Staff) and General Sir Richard Shirreff (former Deputy Supreme Allied Commander EU of NATO). I was also lucky enough to speak to Colonel Chris Hadfield, former

Commander of the International Space Station, who talked to me about leadership in extreme environments. I learned a lot from my conversation with entrepreneur Tony Hsieh about leading an incredibly fast-scaling business, and with Carlo Ancelotti, one of the world's most successful football managers.

What does it mean to be a leader?

General Stanley McChrystal: People often define leadership as influencing people to do things. I think it's a little different than that. Leadership is about creating an environment where people who work with (or for) you can all do better than they would do alone, or in a lesser environment. Leadership is about creating a culture of enablement – that's not about rubbing everyone on the stomach and being nice, but about helping people make real contributions.

Tony Hsieh: I try to avoid the word leadership. If you imagine a greenhouse as being a metaphor for a typical company, the plants in the greenhouse could be considered the employees, and the tallest, strongest plant that all the other employees aspire to be, that's the CEO. That's not how I think of my role; I'm the architect of the greenhouse, and my job is to create an environment that enables growth and flourishment. I see my role more as trying to create the right environment, context and systems to enable employees to really be the best they can be and find that intersection between what they're passionate about and what they're good at! I never set out to find a better or worse way to run a business; it was really just more about what works for my personality and what I'm interested in. Years ago, I used to throw lots of events and parties. I would try and think about things like what else was on in town that evening, what bars would be open en route, their opening times, and everything I could in order to get the circulation and flow for my guests. I was never the centre of attention or life of the party. Once the party's going, I just kind of enjoyed being there in the background and watching the flow. I guess it's kind of the same way I think about a company.

General Richard Myers: Nothing good really gets done in life without somebody taking a lead and organizing people to do something meaningful for society. To me, a leader is the one who organizes teams to meet a mission or some specific goal. A leader is the one who is able to get people moving in the same direction in a collaborative environment to get things done. A lot of people think that military leaders just bark out orders, and I wish they could have followed me around when I was Chairman of the Joint Chiefs of Staff. I didn't command anybody, so everything had to be done through persuasion and collaboration.

General Sir Richard Shirreff: Leadership is about getting people to do willingly, and well, what we as leaders want them to do. I was a professional soldier for thirty-seven years and leadership is absolutely at the heart of command, and of commanding soldiers. There are many other aspects to leadership in the army, but if you can't lead soldiers, you're never going to be any good as a soldier or as an officer. The selection process for army officers is all about establishing whether or not an individual has the potential to become a leader, and how their natural talent can be combined with the nurture, the training, to ensure their potential is realized.

Stew Friedman: I think about leadership and what it means to be a leader not so much as an aspect of one's position or role in an organization in a hierarchy, but instead as a quality that anyone can embody. The simple definition I use is that leaders mobilize people towards valued goals. They bring people to a better place. And you can do this either very well, with no one reporting to you in a formal hierarchy, or, conversely, very badly when at the top of a pyramid.

Carlo Ancelotti: Leadership is transmitting your goals and objectives to your team and achieving a collective acceptance and understanding of your vision.

Leadership changes with the times; the style of leadership needed in a crisis is perhaps not the same as that which would be required during peacetime. In each case, it's a different set of tools, approaches and qualities that are needed to bring people together. To look specifically at the type of leadership we need in today's world, I talked to Jacqueline Novogratz, one of the world's foremost social-impact investors, Gary Hamel, ranked as the world's leading expert on business strategy, and Robert Reich, who has served during several US administrations.

What is the style of leadership we need for our world?

Jacqueline Novogratz: Many of the leaders who run too many of our institutions (political, financial and social) grew up with a world view formed around divisions. Gender division, economic division, social division, the division between giving and taking. It's perhaps inevitable, therefore, that the tools of leadership we see are command, control and divide rather than collaborate, connect and unite. Today, we're facing acute global health and social crises, and the only way we will solve them is if we protect the vulnerable and collaborate. We need to build a narrative of hope, and a new kind of leadership that encourages us all to thrive. A true, moral leader is one that leads with transparency, honesty and trust.

Robert Reich: We need leaders in the political and public sector who understand the dangers of inequality and corruption. When you have massive inequality and wealth at the top, you almost invariably get corruption. Money is used and abused, and the political culture begins coming apart – distrust mounts, and the very wealthy secede from society. This threatens the common good; if social trust is sacrificed, and those with means secede from society, you no longer have the commons, there is no longer a good. When social distrust mounts, when people feel like the game is rigged against them, they are especially vulnerable to demagogues who come along and want them to channel their rage, anxiety and distrust towards scapegoats who have nothing to do with the underlying problems, but who become easy targets as methods to deflect blame.

Carlo Ancelotti: An individual's leadership style is dependent on that person's character. Leadership style is not learned, but rather an extension of who you are, and there is no 'faking' or trying to be something you are not. Those you are leading quickly see who you are and whether you are genuine.

Do we need to redefine leadership?

Gary Hamel: Nobody has anything like a shared definition of what leadership is. During the Industrial Revolution, we started bringing large numbers of people into the workplace, most of them very poorly educated. You therefore needed a new class of 'uber-employee' to wrangle with all these people, and so we invented the manager. Wharton was established in 1881, Harvard Business School in 1908, as places to train these new managers. At the time, management was a weird, unique, complicated role, somewhat like a data scientist, AI engineer or geneticist would be today. We now have a huge leadership industry that is mostly founded on bullshit, and there is very little statistical evidence that leadership training makes an economic difference to firms.

Leadership is in dire need of a dramatic rethink and my definition of leadership is simple: a leader is someone who plays a catalytic role in collective accomplishment. We have to become internal activists and change systems from within, and if you think about the people who really make a difference in our world, the people who change things, they're almost never people with positional authority. How much positional authority is held by Greta Thunberg? Instead, she has the courage to take on problems bigger than she is. She also has contrarian thinking, meaning that she realizes we need a new point of view because the old system of thinking hasn't yet solved the big problems. Great leaders are also people filled with compassion. They are not in it for themselves, they are not trying to fight their corner and make bureaucratic wins. They are doing it because they feel an ethical and moral responsibility to make a difference and build communities around them. Bureaucracy isn't going to fall from the top; it will fall from underneath when people start to challenge the idea that it's the best way to run an organization. You are only as helpless as you choose to be. We're trained in bureaucracies to hardly wipe our bottoms without first of all asking, 'Hey, is this OK boss?' and that's why you have millions and millions of people who show up every day at work physically, but they're not there with their passion, initiative or creativity.

Are there any essential characteristics to leadership?

General Sir Richard Shirreff: Different people will draw up different characteristics for what constitutes a great leader. For me, physical courage obviously in a military setting, but I would also highlight moral courage – the courage to take difficult decisions and be prepared to speak truth unto power and to look after your people. Integrity is fundamental along with charisma, that ability to communicate to your people and to understand, almost through intuition, through empathy, through emotional intelligence, their thoughts, their fears, their needs. As a leader, you must be able to reassure your team, and make them believe that you can address and look after their concerns, and therefore they're more likely to follow you as a result.

Leading your immediate team can be done with some proximity, but at scale, culture is needed as a medium of transmission for mission values and modes of being. Culture is the playbook that every member of your team, whether 100 or 100,000, will refer to in order to determine how they go about their work. Without exception, the most successful companies in the world have culture at their heart; some, such as Netflix, have even turned their culture into iconic status, codifying it into the 'culture deck' that has become essential reference material for companies around the world, and it is the checkpoint for practically every decision made within the business.

How do you make excellence a part of company culture?

Stephen Schwarzman: At Blackstone, for example, we have regular weekly meetings with important groups. Whether it's your immediate area or not – you will have a large group meeting during the week that brings the whole team together and this is led by our senior management (note, we don't view ourselves as management but rather as players and coaches). The meeting may involve hundreds of people, sometimes via screens all over the world. The group feels like a partnership and ensures people feel they are together looking at the particular opportunities or challenges. Anyone is able to comment on anything, be asked questions and get briefed by key people from economics to government affairs, public relations to legal. To make excellence part of culture, you have to hook everyone into it – and that's how we do it. You also have to treat everyone as equals – what does that mean? Everyone has a stake in doing the right thing, and you have to show people, through example, every week how to be thinking and acting to live that culture, how to live those values of right and wrong, risk management and so on. It's very empowering as a twenty-two-year-old to have access to the same information as someone who's fifty, and been doing the job twenty-five years or longer. The truth is that just because you're younger, it doesn't mean you're not the same in terms of capability or insight – the older people just have a bit more experience. It is techniques like this that have allowed us to grow culture at scale.

How do you build and lead high-performance teams?

Nico Rosberg: First of all, you must realize that a team is always stronger than a single individual. You cannot win a championship by just being a great driver. You must have a very good team behind you. This is the same in every business. In the past year, I have grown a team of about twenty employees working for me permanently and I have taken great care in choosing young people with diverse skills, an innovative mindset and the ability to think outside the box. I learn from them every day and this is an important lesson, too. As a leader, you are not infallible. It is important to be able to admit a lack of expertise in certain areas of your business and to rely on your team's expertise instead. This also frees up your mind to think about the bigger picture.

Carlo Ancelotti: It has always been important to me to try to establish a personal relationship with each one of my players. To find a place where we communicate and have a mutual exchange. I often try to speak with my players in their native language, as it immediately breaks down barriers.

How did you build a company with deeply embedded values?

Hamdi Ulukaya: I was 100 per cent outside the business environment when I started out. I'd never worked anywhere, I'd never known anyone who started a business, I didn't know any CEOs, I had no business 'network', I'd never studied business. I was just an ordinary person who saw being the CEO of a successful business as being something in the far distance. When I started out, I had one thing on my mind: I didn't want to be the person I hated when I was growing up. I also had a real passion to bring this factory back to life, to make it sustainable once again. It was closed down by a large food manufacturer, and I saw how much the community suffered and how many people were left behind. This giant company destroyed a community from a distance, and it hit the nerve of everything I hated about the way business was done. I wanted to bring the factory back, but I didn't want to follow in their footsteps – I wanted to do things better. I had to find a new way, with a new playbook, in my own environment without the world watching.

We were small, we had old equipment, we didn't even know if it was going to work out. What I did have was a connection to the reality of people. I believed in human qualities, where your handshake meant something, where you could trust your colleague, and they'd have your back, where everyone was in it together with the same spirit. This community was similar to where I grew up, it was the same feeling, and I wanted to start the journey from that place where everybody felt important, everyone felt at home.

How do you build trust?

Jacqueline Novogratz: Trust is the rarest currency we have; and it's the most precious. Learning to build and give trust isn't easy – and takes practice. I started Acumen in April 2001. Six months later, it was 9/11. I had a team of four people – we were moving into our offices, right next door to Ground Zero in New York. I asked my team, 'What do we do now?' I really felt this was going to be a moment where the world pulls inwards instead of thinking globally. So, I pulled together a table of the best experts I could find on the Taliban, extremism and terrorism and at the end of the night someone said, 'If you were king, what would you do?' Glibly, I said, 'I would go to the Muslim world and find those individuals who are building civil society institutions that could build trust and opportunity inside the community and show the world outside what was possible too.' A funder gave us a million-dollar cheque, and I literally went to my team and said, 'Right, where do we begin?'

Carlo Ancelotti: My relationships are based on mutual respect. I first give respect and then ask for it in return. I also believe in trusting my players to give their best on and off the pitch. However, I must give the group direction and therefore need to be the collective voice. If my respect or trust is violated, there needs to be consequences.

How can leaders effectively change behaviours?

John Kotter: We are in a world that is changing faster than ever, and if the rate of change inside your business is slower than the rate of change outside your business, you're in trouble. Organizations have to change; the most fundamentally complicated aspect of that is the behaviour of their employees. People get into jobs, habits and cultures that in general are born out of the tendency for organizations to reach equilibrium. Organizations tend to have a lot of hierarchy, policy and procedures, the aim being 'to get the trains running on time'. Against that backdrop, it's difficult to figure out how to accommodate changes, from the mundane to the disruptive, from changing train schedules to someone like Uber changing everything.

Leadership is the need to change things for the better and that starts with people. It's about figuring out how to get a group of people, in particular circumstances, to keep moving forward. It's about that grand vision for the future, and getting people to move in a single, unified, direction. It's about creating conditions that engage, empower and energize so you can keep pace with the world outside you. Management is about processes and procedures that keep trains running on time. It's about planning, systems, budgeting systems, organizational structure, HR and so on. Today's organizations are struggling to change direction fast and it's because they just don't have enough people taking leadership roles throughout their structures. Leadership is a set of actions, it's a behaviour, and one that can be adopted by anyone in an organization. Leadership helps firms become social movements, but if you said that to most managers, they simply wouldn't understand it.

What does power mean to leaders?

General Stanley McChrystal: Power can be positional, reputational, financial and so many other things, but the bottom line is this: it gives the leader leverage. It gives the leader the ability to get things done, or to force some things which can cause more people to be willing to interact with them or follow them. If you look at who has the power in today's world, a certain percentage will be people with money, and many others will have created a persona, or have resources that create a following. Power is much more subtle than simply the ability to give orders. Leaders have the ability to create a shared consciousness built on consensus. That's the strongest power there is – it creates a multiplier effect.

General Richard Myers: As Chairman of the Joint Chiefs of Staff, it meant that I was the highest-ranking individual in the US military, a position which people assume has great power. I never thought about power, though. I didn't dream about it, think about it. My job was fulfilling our responsibilities to the security of our nation, our friends and allies. It was collaborating, generating better ideas, better plans and better strategies. It was about looking after our people and getting the mission done. When the law says you're the most senior military person in the United States, people respect that – you don't need to say anything about it, you just have to get the job done. If people over emphasize power, they will forget a lot of things which make leaders effective, including the most critical relationships. Who wants to follow some leader on a power trip? Nobody! Good leaders have to find ways to put their ego way off to the side and work on building relationships, building credibility, building trust.

How do you negotiate?

Mark Cuban: When I negotiate, I don't try to win, I try to get to my goal. The best deal is the one where everyone feels like they've left something on the table; and I'm good with that. When I negotiate, I try to look at the business I'm negotiating with and think, 'If I were them, if I owned their business, what would I be looking for? What's important to me? What do their numbers tell me? What's the culture of their organization?' I try to put myself in their shoes to understand their position. On *Shark Tank*, you get ten minutes of it as a viewer, but in real time those sessions can be two hours long, so it gives you time to lift the lid. One of the things I'm good at is getting to the heart of the matter quickly. I can walk into any type of business, get to know it after a few questions, and can understand how to improve it – usually with technology. *Shark Tank* is the same thing – I listen to the entrepreneurs, get to the core of their business, and understand their position. In my mind, I need to understand who they are, what they need, what's important to them and what their perspectives are. Knowing that allows me to understand where I think they can or can't draw the line.

Running a business is a paradox; it's simultaneously the best and worst career choice you could possibly make. Every single day is an adventure. It's a cliché, but rarely do you have two days that are the same and it's opened doors and opportunities for me that I could never have expected. Running a business can also be one of the loneliest, most challenging, soul-destroying and stressful jobs, particularly when a business fails – it hurts, no two ways about it. But when it's going well, I wouldn't change it for the world. In my own career, I have almost certainly failed more than I've succeeded in terms of numbers of projects, but as an entrepreneur you hope that the successes return you more than your failures have absorbed. It's not just an entrepreneurship reality, it's a leadership reality: the higher you go in any career, the more complex your decision-making environment is, the more relationships, stakeholders and dependencies each decision will impact on, and, often, the more gravity each decision carries. To expect failure not to occur is therefore a fallacy; the most important thing is to put failure in context and to learn from it.

What is the role of failure in leadership?

Mark Cuban: Failure is painful. You have to learn from it. I've learned more from the jobs I've got fired from than the jobs that I liked. Every company I've failed, I've learned. It doesn't matter how many times you fail – you only have to be right once. That's all it takes to be an overnight success. People don't remember your failures. When it happens, you feel like you can't walk outside, you feel like people are staring at you every day, questioning you, judging you. You think you are a failure. That's never the case. Let me tell you the honest-to-God truth about how your friends and stakeholders see your failure. Within thirty days, they've forgotten about it. Ask yourself about all your friends, all the entrepreneurs that you've ever met, all the businesses you've ever seen that failed. You can barely remember them. You certainly don't have any strong opinions about them. You don't really care! It's like breaking up with a significant other: it's painful – but you'll get over it.

General Stanley McChrystal: I was recently with a group who asked me, 'In wartime, are people scared of failure?' and the answer sometimes surprises people. In wartime, people are much more afraid of failure than physical harm. For leaders, fear of failure is hugely important. If you look at the negative behaviours of many organizations and people, they are as a result of dodging responsibilities and decisions through a fear of failure. Fear of failing limits organizations. A little bit of fear is good, it generates a creative tension and gets people to respect the task at hand, but as soon as you're more scared of failure than you are excited about succeeding, that's when fear becomes a problem. Organizations have to train and condition people to understand what the risks really are, and how to not be terrified by them. You have to look at risk as individuals, teams, organizations and even at the existential. You have to make sure people in your organization are not scared of failing, and don't feel there's a checklist of who's failed X amount of times. You have to look at who accomplishes, who succeeds, and realize that there will be a percentage of failure needed to get there. You have to focus on who makes a difference, and that's not always measured by money.

Colonel Chris Hadfield: The role of failure depends on the purpose of your team. If you're on a chess team, losing a match may cause disappointment for you and your team, but it will not cause a tragedy. If you're a team of astronauts trying to dock with a space station, failure most likely means death or, at best, significant financial and mission consequences. The higher the stakes, the more important it is to realize that failure is inevitable and so we have to anticipate it, prepare for it, minimize it and, ideally, avert it. We have to embrace failure into our practice of leadership; it is inevitable and, frankly, if everything went right, we wouldn't need leaders! It's important too that we look at our language around it; perhaps instead of calling it failure, it makes more sense to call it the opposite of going right, i.e. going wrong. Understanding failure means practising when consequences are low. For example, if a fireman messes up during a real fire, there could be loss of life. This is why they use realistic simulations to practise processes, prevent errors happening and understand the real world more accurately. Ultimately, even if you practise a complex task dozens of times, you may not be perfect, but you will significantly increase your chances of succeeding when things go wrong. In our day-to-day lives this happens too. Think about heart attacks; they are a common medical emergency. There's a chance that many of us will, at some point in our lives, come across someone having a heart attack, but if you did, do you know what you would do in that situation? This is something we can all practically prepare for, perhaps with some online research, or by taking a first-aid course.

What do success and failure mean to you?

Nico Rosberg: My whole life was dominated by success and the fear of failure. Success is like a drug. Once you have tasted it, you want more. Fear, on the other hand, is a huge mind blocker as it kills your self-confidence and creativity. So, I have learned to deal with these emotions through meditation and psychological coaching during my time in F1. It is important to find a balance, become aware of negative thought patterns and control your mind more proactively. I have become much better at that and, of course, today I define success differently. I have proven that I can win a Formula One World Championship. This feeling will carry me for ever.

Carlo Ancelotti: Success for me is when my team plays in unison and is one. When there is cohesion in the style of play, I have done my job in transmitting my ideas to my players. However, there are many extraneous factors necessary for success in football and whether the team plays well or not can be seen as less important when winning is paramount. Regardless, I believe that with a collective understanding of what is expected of each player, the chances of success are higher. Failure is an important tool with which one can reassess and reconstruct an idea or process. It is an essential element of the feedback loop. Failure should be used to step back and question your method and weaknesses. To recognize failure early can ultimately make one much stronger down the road.

Do we need to redefine success?

Jacqueline Novogratz: Our notion of success, set by our parents, our families, our friends and educational institutions, can hold us back. The whole world has defined success as being money, fame and power. And while that has enabled a few people to get very wealthy, famous and powerful – it has not worked for the many. In the late 1990s, I was in Bangladesh and I was speaking to an older man about the tools of business, and how they can create change. He said, 'I find this challenging – I come from a lineage of poets.' At the time it was the poets, storytellers and intellectuals who were praised by society; those in business were seen as a little 'dirty' and so, for him, the shift in culture from business being seen as dirty to being primary for success was a big deal. Today, at this time of Covid, in parts of the world where business is everything, we're seeing a resurgence of poetry and art as speaking to us. It's easy to forget, but the system isn't something else – we are the system, we define the system. And we will only build systems in which all of us can flourish if we redefine what success means in terms of a shared humanity and sustainability, and not money, power and fame.

How do you bring a culture of being 'in it together' across success and failure?

Stephen Schwarzman: Whenever you look at creating anything, whether that's a new investment or organization, there will be risks. The key to having something succeed is to make sure you know and manage those risks. In an ideal world, you don't want to be taking risks. There is a common myth that entrepreneurs are risk-takers. If you ask entrepreneurs, they tell you they're not – why would you take a risk on something you didn't think was going to work? Smart entrepreneurs create processes that virtually eliminate risk to the extent that it would be taken. In our world, it's very common that organizations have one great person interrogating a team or idea to determine if something is worth pursuing. The outcome of this is that you're hostage to one person's views – and they could be wrong. At Blackstone, we've built a model that we feel is optimized around managing risk in decision-making. We have a team of around, say, eight people around the table. They have written materials that describe the situation and risks, and have a value that says that if you eliminate all risk, the upside takes care of itself. The principle is that everyone at the table participates, there are no dominant people. Each person has to discuss the risks of losing money, and how not to. I'm a great believer in not losing money – it's not profound, but it's enduring.

The team itself is not responsible for the success or failure of the project. Everyone has discussed it, everyone is aware of the risks, and if something goes wrong, 90 per cent it will be one of the risks that has been identified, and that means that all of us have mis-assessed that risk. By having an objective process, you support your people, avoid blame culture and give a very secure environment to have intellectual, analytical engagement. In life, your response to failure is much more important than your response to success. It sounds counterintuitive, but it's not. Your job as a manager or a leader is to figure out what went wrong, and to fix it, and make sure it doesn't happen again. That's how you build great organizations, not by burying mistakes but by talking openly about them.

⚙�⚙

These days, I'm largely OK, but I have battled with anxiety and depression for decades. At times I have been sufficiently low to contemplate (and attempt) ending it all. I know I'm not alone in feeling this way – every forty seconds someone, somewhere, tries to take their own life. By the time you get to the end of this sentence, three people will most likely have tried, and one will most likely have succeeded. For me, it was severe anxiety – probably caused by work – which resulted in depression, which I avoided tackling because, as a CEO and founder, you are expected to display almost superhuman strength and endurance at all times, and mental fortitude a degree beyond what mere mortals could muster – or so I thought. Only when it was close to being too late did I reach out, get help, and begin a journey of recovery that I should have started a decade sooner. As I tell my MBA students each and every year, the single most important life skill they can deploy is resilience.

What is the role of resilience in leadership?

Jocko Willink: Is resilience important to leaders? Of course it is. You're going to fail, you're going to fall flat on your face, you're going to get rejected, you will go off course. All of those things are going to happen, and if you don't have resilience, you are not going to be able to do the necessary to accomplish whatever it is you're trying to accomplish. Listen, I was never that good at anything – I wasn't a great athlete, I wasn't the smartest guy, and so once I got into the SEAL team, the only way for me to perform well was to work hard. I was going to fail, and I had to keep trying and keep working hard – that was the habit that would make me able to do whatever I wanted to do. Building resilience is a decision. You got rejected – what's your decision? You can decide to go knock on another door, or to curl up in a little ball and cry. My recommendation is that you go knock on another door, and you try again. I'm not saying that you won't feel like you want to curl up and cry – and if you want to, go do that, and once you've finished crying, get up, go knock on another door and keep trying. That's resilience. I'm sure there's some philosophical esoteric speech that somebody could find about how to build resilience. Here's how you build resilience: get up and go do what you need to do to get this job done.

How are our lifestyles impacting on our mental health?

Professor Green: Life is high pressure, and the stresses we are all under are getting more and more. We're only designed to have two responses to stress – fight or flight – and that's because we evolved from our ancestors, the hunter-gatherers. Now we have relationship stress, work stress, stress about our friends, about our families, financial stress, mortgage stress, stress about our food. There's a lot that people need to cope with now, and people don't take time to deal with the stress they're going through, even though that stress can cause serious health problems now, and in the future.

Why do our business cultures dismiss sleep?

Arianna Huffington: The glamorization of sleep deprivation is deeply embedded in our culture. Everywhere you turn, sleep deprivation is celebrated, from 'You snooze, you lose' to highly burned-out people boasting, 'I'll sleep when I'm dead.' The combination of a deeply misguided definition of what it means to be successful in today's world – that it can come only through burnout and stress – along with the distractions and temptations of a 24/7-wired world, has imperilled our sleep as never before. It goes back to the Industrial Revolution when sleep became just another commodity to be exploited as much as possible.

Our workdays, especially in the afternoon, have a way of taking on a survivalist tinge – how, we ask ourselves, are we going to make it through the rest of the day, trekking with flagging energy through enemy territory mined with meetings, emails and expanding to-do lists? So we squirrel away provisions – usually unhealthy ones – and, like addicts, we think about where that next shot of caffeine or that next sugar bomb is going to come from. But there are other options. Rather than reach for our fifth cup of coffee or third doughnut to deal with the usual post-lunch lull, consider a twenty- or thirty-minute nap. Perhaps those in the world of business who equate sleep with laziness or lack of dedication can be convinced of the benefits of sleep by looking at what's going on in a world that is the ultimate in pragmatism, where performance and winning are everything: sports. To professional athletes, sleep is not about spirituality, work–life balance, or even health and wellbeing; it's all about performance. It's about what works, about using every available tool to increase the chances of winning.

What did you learn about resilience, focus, competition and success from your career in F1, and how does that apply to the business world?

Nico Rosberg: I have learned a lot in F1 that I can apply to the business world. The biggest lesson is certainly the ability to get the most out of myself and reach my potential. Since my athletic career, I have dealt a lot with methods of personal self-optimization and self-development, be it through mental training, nutrition, meditation or course fitness. This is also very useful outside of competitive sports. For example, since my retirement I have rediscovered meditation. Meditation played a huge role in my World Cup title, but then I stopped because I lacked motivation. The mental intensity was completely gone and will never be there again in the same form.

But I have slowly reintroduced the discipline for meditation again into my daily routine and I can feel the benefits. We know that it's good. As a racing driver, I was always extremely structured, and so are our days now. At 8.30 a.m. today I had an hour doing my homework with my daughter; before that, I had meditated and exercised for an hour. These are all lessons that I have learned from my time in Formula One for my life.

How do you begin to learn from adversity and challenges?

Sheryl Sandberg: We have to acknowledge our adversities, raise problems and admit them. If challenges and hardships are something we never talk about, we're never going to take any learnings from them. Things are wrong all the time in companies and often everyone's instincts are to brush things under the rug. Our culture as individuals and companies is to hide problems, and many of our innovations and technologies enable us to do this. We have to fight hard to stop the behaviour.

How does adversity shape who we are?

Sheryl Sandberg: When I'm giving talks, I always say to the audience, 'Raise your hand if you have heard of post-traumatic stress.' Every hand goes up, but when I say, 'Raise your hand if you've heard of post-traumatic growth,' no hands go up. The data are pretty compelling that there is more post-traumatic growth than there is post-traumatic stress.

The need for resilience is completely unavoidable. We all face challenges big and small in our lives. Even companies are constantly facing the need for resilience as they change shape and form. The real question is: how do we build the muscles for resilience within ourselves, and each other? Businesses too have to realize that resilience is something we build together. We can do it, we have to do it – and we must be methodical and explicit.

Why is it important to hold opposing moral or cultural values in tension?

Jacqueline Novogratz: Throughout history, the moral code in society was often handed down from some higher authority. That may have created strong communities, but it comes at the cost of individuality. Today, we have so much individualism that we've lost a sense of belonging. We've lost a sense of what we share and that's why we have to apply moral imagination to be open to understanding the belief systems and cultures of others, not to instantly assume one is better than the other. We have to navigate moral and cultural differences and make principled decisions against the immutable values of our shared human dignity and the understanding that my actions have an impact on who you are, and what your situation is – and could become. This is not moral relativism where you may say that a culture honours 'honour' more than honesty, and so corruption is morally accepted. In an interdependent world, certain actions such as corruption must be universally not accepted. But in other areas you will find values that are held up as important by a community and which you have to navigate.

Right now, we as a society are choosing between health and the economy. It is not an either/or. We must get above that wall – we have to transcend it and look at how we hold opposing truths in such a way that we can make hard decisions, be transparent, authentic and supportive. This is not about you being right, or me being wrong; it's about finding a truth we can agree on.

Are leaders born or made?

Colonel Chris Hadfield: The randomness of evolution means that everyone is born with strengths and weaknesses; every human being, every dog, every tree. It's certainly true that some people may have a predisposition to want to take some sort of leadership role while others don't, but nobody is perfect at leading, or uniquely born into it. All of us are raw material, and that means we can improve and get better at leading. You often find that in extreme situations, perhaps a fire, or where someone may have a medical emergency. In those situations we find leadership skills we perhaps never knew we had. Leadership is about being willing to enact change – it means saying, 'OK, I'm going to take responsibility for changing something,' and that may be something singular within your own life, or something that affects countless people.

I was just a teenager when I first became interested in leadership. I realized it's the art of influencing human behaviour to accomplish a mission in a manner desired by the leader. I was not born to become a leader by any means. Like all of us, I was born with the raw material to read and observe, and it's almost entirely due to the training I've had, through observing good and bad leaders, and through making room for introspection to decide the things in my life that were worth taking a stand on, that I became a leader. We all have the capacity to lead within us, that's the beauty of leadership – you can do this aged eight or eighty-eight, there's no limit.

As I write this, the world is facing one of its greatest economic and social challenges in peacetime: the Covid-19 pandemic. From a commercial perspective, domestic and global markets have ground to a halt, and the majority of businesses are facing uncertainty, stress and extraordinary volatility. As a leader, it is impossible for you to make long-term strategic decisions during a time like this – you have to adapt your leadership posture to deal with a crisis, and make the next best decision you can with your team – rather than the best strategic decisions *for* your team.

How do leaders deal with incomplete information?

Jocko Willink: Instead of making big giant decisions, I try to make the smallest decision I possibly can that is in the right direction – my best guess. If I want to know whether someone's behind the door, instead of just blasting it open I'd take a step back, crack the door open a little, shine a light in and look. Did I see movement? If not, I'll maybe open the door some more. Eventually, I'll get to a point where I can look inside almost the entire room, and I haven't stepped in yet. Then I can look and see if there are any traps, tripwires, and finally – when I've done everything I can – I can step in the room and see what's there.

Making the smallest decisions I can makes me seem super-decisive, but I'm actually just making really small decisions.

It's the same in the business world. If you're wanting to go explore a new market, you don't just go in and buy three buildings and a hundred people. You start with a kiosk, then maybe two, then maybe three, then maybe you lease a building, and then maybe you buy a building. You don't just jump in. To succeed at decision-making, make iterative decisions and small decisions. The smallest decisions you can in your direction of travel.

Colonel Chris Hadfield: Leaders work with insufficient and incomplete information. Nobody ever has all the information they need to make a decision, and so your own personal competence is key; you need to have the ability to make judgement calls with incomplete information. Take the captain of an aircraft carrier. At any given moment in time, they will not have all the information they need, but they also weren't randomly given the job of commanding that ship. By the time they command a multibillion-dollar aircraft carrier with so many lives on the line, they will have already had a lifetime gaining the practical, technical and academic experience to be able to make decisions when they need to – whether to change course, whether to recover aircraft, whether there is a threat.

As a leader, you have to have a relentless dissatisfaction with your own levels of competence, and a relentless wish to learn and self-improve. We can all learn and score 100 per cent on a test, but if you do that same test six months from now, you will not get that score; you may have forgotten, the system will have changed, the rules may have changed, or you may have changed. No system is fixed, and the more senior you are, the more important it is to be relentless in your approach to self-improvement around your technical knowledge and leadership competence.

During my time on the space station, I remember an incident where we started rapidly spewing liquid ammonia out into space. We had a very limited time to make lots of decisions and to fix this before we ran out of the main coolant needed for the ship. We didn't have enough information, and so we had to go with our hastily assembled plan, based on years of preparation and experience. Every single person on the ship was spacewalk qualified. We'd been studying systems for our entire careers and so we had the mix of understanding and small delicate skills needed to solve a major problem that was not inevitable to solve. Even with all our training, there was absolutely no guarantee of being able to fix this problem – it was not one we had ever simulated – but it was because of our training and professional preparation that we made the repair in record time.

General Sir Richard Shirreff: One of the core pillars of command is that you have to make the right decisions, in a timely manner, when faced with incomplete information. This is something you develop as a leader through training, through education and, most of all, experience. You develop intuition, that gut sense that now is the moment. The military has a principle that you don't move on to the next level of leadership and responsibility until you've proved yourself out of subordinate level. So as an officer, your first appointment is to command a platoon of thirty men or women. You then, after more experience, more training, more education, perhaps command a company which has got four platoons. In time, you might command a battalion or regiment which has got four or five companies. And if you prove yourself at that, you might go on to be a brigade commander which has got again four or five regiments. You're always having to prove yourself at different levels. As leaders we need to have the thinking, training and education, but the practice is critical and that's as relevant to a great business leader as it is to a soldier or anybody in any sector, I think.

What is the role of business in society?

Hamdi Ulukaya: I think the role of business is to lift humanity and push it forward. I truly believe that; not just because of the innovations and products that businesses create, but because of the communities they impact, the people they interact with, and the environment they exist in. I grew up thinking businesses just make money for shareholders and everyone else suffers; whether that is their employees, community or the environment. I grew up hating that idea and I didn't want to be the thing I hated. My own experience in the last ten to twelve years has been that business is an amazing platform to make the world better, from every aspect.

Leadership is not about standing at the front shouting orders; it's about enablement and growth of a team. In many ways, leaders are the glue that holds a team together as it moves towards a goal or objective, or indeed navigates a crisis. The greatest leaders also have a level of humility and self-awareness that allows them to understand their strengths and weaknesses, respond constructively to failure and, perhaps most importantly, work to build resilient teams.

As John Kotter explains, leadership is that essence that brings together a group of people, in a circumstance or context, to move forward towards a vision in a unified manner. It sounds simple, but it is truly remarkable. The fact that we as individuals place our trust in a small group of people to lead us is an incredible by-product of evolution, without which it would have been practically impossible for us to move on from being small groups of nomads into civilizations.

To truly understand leadership, however, we must come back to that difficult realization that we are highly intelligent, yet tribal animals. We have the ability to act and direct our own behaviours, but live in a society with complex structures that require us to cooperate as groups, often at scale. Several of the military professionals in this chapter have seen leadership at work in one of the most extreme environments – war – and described not only how essential leadership is to the human condition, but how essential it is for leaders to deeply understand the individuals and groups for whom they are responsible, so that they can be sure in their communication, and sure in what those under their leadership will do next. The most effective way we have found to counter the disintegration that could arise from us all pursuing our own ends is the existence of centres of authority as leaders.

Thus, the paradox between our need for individual agency and our nature as social animals is resolved. Our plurality means we are not members of a single tribe or group, but rather we are members of families, ethnicities, economic organizations, universities, businesses, friendship circles, sports teams and many more assemblies, all driven around shared goals, visions and interests. It is this nature of our ability to form, lead and direct that has been at the heart of every single major advance – and backwards step – of our species, from our scientific and cultural leaps, to wars and atrocities. It is under leadership that we have been able to walk on the moon, fight disease and improve the living standards of billions; and it is also under leadership that millions exist under brutal regimes.

 **BIOGRAPHIES**

Carlo Ancelotti OSI is an Italian former professional footballer, now manager of English Premier League football club Everton. He is one of only three managers to have won the UEFA Champions League three times, and one of only two to have managed teams in four finals.

Mark Cuban is an American entrepreneur and television personality. He is one of the main investors on the reality television series *Shark Tank*, and is the owner of the NBA team the Dallas Mavericks.

Professor Stew Friedman is the founding director of the Wharton Leadership Program and Wharton's Work/Life Integration Project. He is also a professor at the University of Pennsylvania and hosts a weekly radio show on Sirius XM.

Professor Green (real name Stephen Manderson) is an English rapper, songwriter and television personality. He co-hosts *Lip Sync Battle UK*, has written a bestselling autobiography and is the patron of Calm, a suicide prevention charity.

Colonel Chris Hadfield is a retired astronaut and was the first Canadian to walk in space. He was NASA's Director in Russia, flew three space missions and served as Commander of the International Space Station.

Gary Hamel is an American management speaker, author and celebrated business thinker. He has worked with the London Business School for over thirty years and his books have been translated into over twenty-five languages.

Tony Hsieh is an entrepreneur, venture capitalist and CEO of the online clothing company Zappos. He also co-founded the internet advertising network LinkExchange, which he sold to Microsoft for $265 million in 1998, when he was twenty-five.

Arianna Huffington is an author, columnist and founder of *The Huffington Post*, as well as founder and CEO of Thrive Global, a leading behaviour change tech company.

Professor John Kotter is a professor at Harvard Business School, a bestselling author and founder of the management consulting firm Kotter International.

General Stanley McChrystal is a retired United States army general and founder of the McChrystal Group. Since his retirement he has taught International Relations at Yale University.

General Richard Myers is a retired four-star general in the United States Air Force and currently serves as the fourteenth president of Kansas State University. In his previous role as Chairman of the Joint Chiefs of Staff, he was the highest-ranking uniformed officer of the US military.

Jacqueline Novogratz is a bestselling author, founder and CEO of Acumen, a non-profit organization that invests in leaders and businesses who are enabling people living in poverty to transform their lives, and was named one of the world's 100 Greatest Living Business Minds by *Forbes*.

Professor Robert Bernard Reich is an American economist, bestselling author and political commentator, who served in the administrations of presidents Gerald Ford, Jimmy Carter and Bill Clinton, and was a member of President Barack Obama's economic transition advisory board.

Nico Rosberg is a German-Finnish former racing driver and entrepreneur. He won the 2016 Formula One World Championship and was inducted into the FIA Hall of Fame in 2017.

Sheryl Sandberg is Chief Operating Officer of Facebook, founder of LeanIn.Org, and a philanthropist. She was also the first woman to serve on Facebook's board and has been named by *Time* magazine as one of the most influential people in the world.

Stephen Schwarzman is an American businessman, investor and philanthropist. He is the Chairman and CEO of The Blackstone Group, a global private equity firm and ranked one hundredth on the *Forbes* list of billionaires.

General Sir Richard Shirreff is a retired senior British Army officer and author, who served as Deputy Supreme Allied Commander Europe from 2011 to 2014.

Hamdi Ulukaya is founder, Chairman and CEO of Chobani, one of the fastest-growing food companies in the last decade and a pioneer for the natural food movement.

Jocko Willink is a retired officer of the United States Navy, who served in the Navy SEALs for twenty years. He is a *New York Times* bestselling author and hosts a weekly podcast: the *Jocko Podcast*.

ON ENTREPRENEURSHIP: THE CREATORS AND THE MAKERS

'I believe all human beings are entrepreneurs at the core. It is in our DNA.'

MUHAMMAD YUNUS

I didn't know what an entrepreneur was until I was called one. I was fifteen years old and sitting in a teacher's office at school. Rather than being reprimanded (perhaps the usual reason I would have been there), I was on a call with a local journalist – something the school had organized once they had found out that, since I was about fourteen, I'd been quietly running a business while still at school. The journalist asked me, 'So how does it feel to be a young entrepreneur?' and I panicked! What did that mean? Luckily, the teacher came to my rescue and scribbled on a bit of paper in front of me, 'It just means a businessperson!'

The truth is, entrepreneurship is much more than 'just' anything. For me, the differences between an entrepreneur and a businessperson centre upon the thesis of the venture, the scale and the impact. From the incandescent light bulb to the smartphone, there is very little of our day-to-day lives that has not come about as the result of an entrepreneur with a great idea. Take the former CEO of Microsoft, Steve Ballmer, for example; he was employee number thirty at Microsoft, the first business manager hired by Bill Gates, and a ferociously capable entrepreneur in his own right. Microsoft was built on the idea that every home should have a computer, was scaled to become a global business to enable this, and went on to revolutionize practically every part of our lives as a result. Microsoft's operating system was, in effect, the platform on which the early technology revolution was built.

Entrepreneurs are also navigators. They can find the tailwind, and a path through the headwind. Steve Case, co-founder of AOL, identified the tailwinds of reducing the costs of and increasing demand for internet connectivity, navigated the headwinds of regulations and corporate competitors, and built AOL – the company that truly disrupted internet connectivity during the 1990s. Today, the tailwinds are stronger than ever. Processing power, the capability of software, hardware and connectivity, are all increasing exponentially, enabling entrepreneurs to scale faster than ever before. Some of the greatest beneficiaries of this acceleration are the 'big five': Facebook, Apple, Google, Amazon and Microsoft – in the decade from 2010 to 2020 they grew from a combined 196,000 employees to over 1.25 million. Just picking Amazon out of this pack, their valuation (as of March 2020) of approximately US$1 trillion is larger than the combined valuation of Walmart, Best Buy, Macys, Target, Costco, Gap, Home Depot, Starbucks, Foot Locker, Office Depot and JC Penney. Technology is allowing business to scale faster and larger than at any time in human history; it would previously have taken perhaps an entire generation for companies to achieve what some of these businesses have in just a decade. From the light bulb to the smartphone, from many of our most important medicines to some of our most loved and mundane everyday requirements, there is very little around us that does not have foundations in an entrepreneurial pursuit, a creative and forward-thinking individual who had the vision, tenacity and execution capability to make their ideas a reality.

In this chapter, we will meet some of the most interesting, impactful and inspiring entrepreneurs in the world. From technology to retail, medicine to engineering, these individuals have built and run multibillion-dollar businesses, become tremendously wealthy themselves, created tens of thousands of jobs, and made an impact on the world. Some are household names, others you may never have heard of, but all of them have achieved in a lifetime what most would see as impossible. When I spoke to some of the world's leading entrepreneurs, I always wanted to begin the conversation with the fundamental question of what entrepreneurship actually is. All those I spoke to have been described in their careers as entrepreneurs, but my firm belief remains that the experience and nature of 'what' entrepreneurship is remains not just subjective, but highly variable based on industry and context. I have met entrepreneurs who built incredible businesses during recessions, where there was no other choice but to start something, and I have met others who had that quintessential 'bolt of inspiration' with an idea that they just couldn't let go.

What does entrepreneurship mean to you?

Richard Branson: Entrepreneurship is about taking risks, pushing boundaries, and not being afraid to fail. I tend to go with my gut feeling and by personal experience. If I relied on accountants to make decisions, I most certainly would have never gone into the airline business, most certainly would not have gone into the space business, and I certainly wouldn't have gone into most of the businesses that I'm in. In hindsight, it seems to have worked pretty well to my advantage!

Robin Li: I have a strong desire to do what I like to do. I believe that whether it's innate, or it's something that wells up later in life, the urge to entrepreneurship only bears fruit when you plant the seeds at the intersection of passion and ability – the overlap between the things that you love, and the things that you're really good at.

James Dyson: Being an entrepreneur, an inventor, is about having ideas and having the doggedness to see them through. As an inventor your ideas should be based on creating a solution to a problem – a solution which focuses on function over form. When I started to develop the world's first bagless vacuum cleaner, I knew my idea was solving a fundamental problem. Unsurprisingly, other major vacuum cleaner manufacturers did not agree. But I persevered, against the odds, developing the technology and manufacturing it under my own name. This is a trait all entrepreneurs need: the ability to remain committed to your idea and the drive to see it through to fruition.

Muhammad Yunus: An entrepreneur is an initiator, a planner, a result producer, a risk-taker, an organizer. He feels confident about his success. In conventional business an entrepreneur wants to make personal profit. In the conventional sense of business, profit measures his success. In social business, he wants to solve a human problem in a financially sustainable way, without taking personal profit out of it. He gets his investment money back when the business is successful, but doesn't take any dividend after that point. Profit stays with the company to grow. I believe all human beings are entrepreneurs at the core. It is in our DNA.

Kiran Mazumdar-Shaw: Entrepreneurship is really about being self-employed, creating your own path, your own employment journey. It begins with an idea that you want to commercialize; and it's about realizing that it's going to be a pretty challenging process. Entrepreneurship doesn't necessarily come to everyone as a thought, but you can seed it in people's minds, and it becomes something that people can get very excited about! It's not about being born an entrepreneur. I never thought I would run a business! I always call myself an accidental entrepreneur – I was actually passionate about pursuing a career in brewing. Circumstances often become the reason why people become entrepreneurs.

N. R. Narayana Murthy: Entrepreneurship is primarily about a person using their imagination, dreams, daring, sacrifice and passion to create jobs for society, wealth for oneself – and his or her colleagues – and prosperity for the nation. Entrepreneurship is about transforming the world.

Tory Burch: Entrepreneurship is about recognizing a void in the market and having the ability to build a business around it. I didn't realize I was an entrepreneur until I had the concept for our company and started to develop it, but in retrospect I see that I was entrepreneurial in everything I did in my career leading up to that point. It is also about knowing your strengths and weaknesses and surrounding yourself with a stellar team.

Steve Case: At a broad level, entrepreneurship is about having a positive impact on the world. Entrepreneurs are a key avenue to ushering in change, innovation and impact – they challenge the status quo, figure out better ways to doing things, whether that's a product or service, build teams around those ideas and *really* have positive impact. Entrepreneurship is, of course, about businesses, but at its core are innovation and people.

Jerry Yang: For me entrepreneurship means finding a common, strong mission to build something that would have impact, or change the world. While the goal of building a great product or company is very important, the journey of getting there is what I treasure the most. The most enjoyable part of my entrepreneurial journey is going through the ups and downs of building a team. There is nothing like having built a team that shares the same strong passion and beliefs, and mostly sharing that journey of success and failure together. For me, there is some natural risk-taking that I was born with, but so much of being an entrepreneur is also learned – through hard work and the team you are surrounded by.

Jack Welch: If you are an entrepreneur, you have a certain DNA, a certain spirit. As an entrepreneur, if you have an idea, you'll go to the ends of the earth to make it succeed. You'll find every day is a new journey, you're up, you're down, there's a surprise every minute. I don't think entrepreneurship is a profession like doctor or lawyer. I meet so many people on my travels and when I ask them what they want to be, they say, 'entrepreneur'. Wait a minute, it's not a profession. Entrepreneurship is something in your DNA. If you have an idea and the passion to make it win, you're an entrepreneur. Not everyone has that DNA, and that's OK!

Steve Ballmer: There are two kinds of entrepreneurship people talk about: starting something new, like a new company, or doing something new from inside something established. To me it comes down to the same thing regardless of setting – big company, small company, not for profit, for profit – you will see a pattern that will let you believe you are seeing something others aren't seeing, and you will summon the energy, brain power and commitment to bring in others and make it into something. It is taking risk to do that, which is part of entrepreneurship, and there are plenty of ways of doing that without starting your own company.

Dennis Crowley: I don't really like the term entrepreneur because I think to some it implies that you start businesses for the sake of starting businesses. My view is this: if there's something you want to see in the world that doesn't exist, go build that thing. If that means you have to build a company? So be it. I give a lot of talks, and always get introduced on stage as being an entrepreneur. One of the first slides I usually show is a quote from Alexis Ohanian, co-founder of Reddit, that says: 'Entrepreneur is just French for "has ideas, does them".' It's actually *not* French for that, but I like Alexis's interpretation.

José Neves: I think the entrepreneurial spirit was always in me. When I was eight, I was given a computer for Christmas. It came with no video games, just a programming manual. I started coding and found my first passion: creating software. In 1993, when I was nineteen, I started my first business. It was a 'software house', creating software for businesses and, being from the north of Portugal and a family with a history of shoemaking, fashion companies naturally became my clients. That's when I found my second passion: fashion. Eventually,

I became a shoe designer, a boutique owner, a tradeshow organizer, a bit of everything in fashion. I fell in love with the industry – I was swept away by its people, places, chaotic creativity. Fashion is all about craftsmanship, creativity and great design. It celebrates beauty in every form. But it's not art. It's supposed to be worn, but more than that, as you wear it, it changes the way you feel that day and helps you to project how you want the world to see you.

Gary Vaynerchuk: To be an entrepreneur, you need a love for process and to be comfortable with adversity. If you love process and you're comfortable with adversity, and if you love the journey over the fruits and riches of that journey, then you have what it takes to be a successful entrepreneur.

Entrepreneurship is on a pedestal; everyone wants to be one. Here's the truth: it sucks. Entrepreneurship is hard and almost everyone loses. You genuinely have to like getting beaten up. You genuinely have to like conflict. You genuinely have to have an enormous amount of patience. This is what it takes to be an entrepreneur and not just play at it.

✿✿

You often hear entrepreneurship referred to as something people are born with – the same hypothesis ascribed to great artists – and this was certainly a view I came across in my various conversations with successful entrepreneurs. In my experience, while there are certainly psychological characteristics that are common to a lot of entrepreneurs – self-efficacy, innovativeness, locus of control, need for achievement, openness, extroversion, agreeableness – there are also a wide range of external factors that perhaps play a more important role: the 'serendipity' of an idea, timing, market conditions, access to capital and –

something not often discussed – exposure to entrepreneurship culturally. My father was a small-business entrepreneur, trading fabrics from his office in Manchester; from an early age, the world of business was demystified for me. Throughout the Indian diaspora, entrepreneurship is a deeply embedded part of culture, and growing up in an Indian household you see the mechanics of business from your earliest days. Perhaps this kind of exposure can equip you with some of the necessary tools to enter that world.

⚙⚙

What is the role of entrepreneurs in an economy and society?

Richard Branson: It's my strong belief that those with the power to help should be encouraged to do exactly that. It's important for entrepreneurs to nurture talent, to provide advice and to provide investment where required. Increasingly, we are hearing more about how big business needs to play its role in society for the greater good. We all have a role to play and it makes business sense. In fact, consumers demand that business be responsible.

Robin Li: Entrepreneurs have been absolutely essential in the transformation of the world we live in. By creating new businesses and new markets, they're real change agents in history. This is something that's been happening for many hundreds of years. As an entrepreneur you have a certain perspective and real motivation to see what's in store for the future. And in trying to anticipate the future, entrepreneurs are chief agents in bringing the future about. It's really been the role of the entrepreneur to take the measure of what people will want in the future, and to change the way people think and behave. They are and will continue to be a vital force in defining the world of the future.

James Dyson: Transport, natural disasters, the distribution of resources, globalization – engineers and inventors have the traits and skill sets to solve the problems the world faces today, and therefore have the potential to impact the world and economy. The economy can be boosted by exporting tangible technology that is in global demand. This is in the hands of engineers.

Muhammad Yunus: Entrepreneurs are innovators. Those who see opportunities have one thing in common – when they see one, they grab it. These opportunities are seen by various types of entrepreneurs in various ways. Personal profit-seeking entrepreneurs see it as an opportunity to make profit for themselves. Some among them could not care less what negative impact their business would produce on the society. Some do care about negative impacts, and want to avoid such businesses. Some want to make money while providing a product or service which is useful to the society, and the planet. Social business entrepreneurs see the opportunity of solving problems of people which are now left to the governments to solve, or never considered to be solvable by anybody – unemployment, for example.

N. R. Narayana Murthy: Entrepreneurs make multiple contributions to society. Firstly, the power of an entrepreneur's ideas adds value to their society. Their ideas may reduce the cost of something, reduce the cycle time of tasks, improve productivity, improve quality of life, and bring new and easier ways of seeking pleasure through leisure products like books, music and videos. Secondly, entrepreneurs create jobs. They use their ideas to create better and more highly paid jobs for their people. Therefore, they create prosperity for society. When you enhance a society's prosperity you don't just create jobs in your own company, industry or sector. You also create job opportunities in the secondary and tertiary sectors. I do not know of any society that has become more prosperous without the power of entrepreneurship. Thirdly, entrepreneurs serve as role models for society through their ability to dream, show courage, take risks, and transform the world around them.

Tony O. Elumelu: I believe that entrepreneurs, like other private sector operators, have an obligation to channel their acumen towards enhancing their social environments, as much as their financial statements. I run an Africapitalist organization, which means that my businesses create value for shareholders and society alike. Personally, I am pleased to see that global leaders now agree that entrepreneurship, not charity, is better able to create progressive, sustainable development that benefits the poor. This is why the United Nations has included the promotion of development-oriented policies that support entrepreneurship in the 2030 Agenda for Sustainable Development. In many developing countries where competing priorities and limited resources can overwhelm government systems, the private sector is uniquely positioned to mobilize the capital assets that can realize lasting, positive social transformation. The relationship between corporation and community is symbiotic: by contributing to raising the standards of living around them, these entrepreneurs are also positioning their businesses to profit from increased disposable incomes, a healthier, better educated pool of potential employees, and numerous other benefits.

What are the key drivers for an entrepreneur?

Richard Branson: It's a combination of passion, vision, creativity and a sense of adventure. I have said on many occasions the reason to start a new business should not be about making money! You need to have a passion for the project and want to make a difference.

Robin Li: I don't think that those who set out to create companies with nothing in mind other than making money are apt to succeed. That's not going to get you out of bed, eager to get to work. It has to come from a higher place. In my case, I knew that I had the ability, through these technologies that I understood well and could confidently implement, to make a real difference in the access ordinary people had to information. And I knew that connecting people to information in the easiest, most convenient way would make a tremendous difference in the world. It wasn't an abstract desire to create. And money is just an afterthought. What drove me to it was this desire to make a difference in an area that badly needed it, and my recognition that I was the right person to step in and take on that challenge.

Muhammad Yunus: I use the word 'entrepreneurship' in the context of personal profit-driven business only. For social business I'll use 'social business entrepreneurship'. Both are entrepreneurship, but of different kinds, leading to different results. One is selfish entrepreneurship, another is selfless entrepreneurship. It is the selfless entrepreneurship which will lead the world to social, economic and environmental sustainability, and create a new civilization of balance between present residents of the world and all future generations.

Chip Wilson: Entrepreneurs get up in the morning and are driven, no matter what, because they know the future is waiting for their idea to be there. When wealth actually comes, you realize that it buys you time – you can hire an executive assistant to do your calendaring and tasks, you can then spend more of your time on the high-functioning elements of your role. The wealthier you become, you maybe look then at jets, chauffeurs, things like that, but ultimately, I need to free up every second of my time to accomplish everything I want to accomplish.

It's fascinating contrasting the views of Muhammad Yunus with those of our other entrepreneurs. Yunus is a pioneer in the field that is now known as social enterprise. He won the Nobel Peace Prize in 2006 for the creation of Grameen Bank, and for creating the engine that allowed millions to lift themselves out of poverty through access to finance. A for-profit business, with a strong social purpose. For many businesses, the traditional model was to make money, do good later, but increasingly now, businesses are realizing that these two paths – making money and doing good – are not separate. You cannot forgo your social, environmental, cultural and human responsibilities to pray at the altar of profit.

Naveen Jain: People measure success in different ways, but whether you look at Bill Gates or Mother Teresa, the thing they have in common is their ability to go out and make a positive impact on the lives of hundreds of millions of people. Success is not about how much money you have in the bank, but rather how many lives have you been able to impact positively. This whole concept of a social entrepreneur has done a disservice to society. To me, the term 'social entrepreneur' is akin to a consolation prize; it's like saying: 'Hey, you could have been a good entrepreneur so let's give you a consolation prize.' Entrepreneurship is social, we are all social entrepreneurs!

Steve Case: The act of taking an idea and making it available to everybody, with scale and impact, is a huge motivator for entrepreneurs. In my own journey, thirty years ago when we started AOL, only 3 per cent of people were online. We thought the world would be better if *everyone* was online, and we set out to do that. It took a decade before we got traction, but we were driven by the idea that living in a more digital and interconnected world would be a good thing for society. Our motivation was partly about building our business, but partly about building this new medium: the internet. That same kind of drive we had is what we see in entrepreneurs we get involved with. It's not just about building a business, it's also about having a real impact in the world.

will.i.am: I've never said, 'Yeah man, we're gonna' be rich!' – money has never been the 'carrot' for me. How do you keep driving forward and doing things? That's what motivates me. I'm like, 'Man, what's next?' What always frustrated the hell out of the Black Eyed Peas about me was that we would be at the Super Bowl, or would have just finished a three-night stadium tour, and I would say, 'Right guys, what's next?' and everybody would be like, 'Ahh, c'mon man, why not just relax?' But I'd be like, 'C'mon, we could do this, we could do that!' My mind just never stopped thinking about what we could be doing next. If we climbed Mount Everest together and we were all at the top, tired, with blisters, dehydrated, I'm the guy who's like, 'Yo! Let's build a freakin' rocket launcher here so we can go to the moon! We're close enough!'

Donna Karan: I'm driven to do what I haven't done. I love a creative challenge, to learn a new craft, a new business, a new way of doing things. The inspiration is always there. Right now, I'm looking out the window at a tree that has white leaves and wondering what I can do with it. Creatively, nature always inspires me. But on a practical level, it's about filling the void, coming up with something that answers the frustration of what's missing, what would make life easier.

One of the most enjoyable aspects of my life now is teaching and I'm lucky enough to be part of visiting faculty at some of the world's highest-rated business schools. Entrepreneurship has generated rock-star figures in business who have the wealth, the power and the reach of any celebrity or icon. So, it is perhaps inevitable that when you put ambitious students in a room to talk about entrepreneurship, they want to know how they can be those icons of the future. Each semester, I get asked what it takes to be a great entrepreneur, and where those ideas emerge from.

What are the characteristics of a great entrepreneur?

Robin Li: I think that only a very small handful of entrepreneurs are 'born' with all the requisite abilities they need to succeed. Most of us have many skills that we've needed to learn along the way. In an incredibly dynamic industry like the internet, you're faced with the constant possibility that you, the disruptor, will quickly become the disrupted. You have to be ready to embrace change, and to be ready for it not just in terms of your business, but psychologically ready for the kind of change – excited by, and attracted to, change itself. I think an entrepreneur needs to have finely tuned sensitivity to what change is coming. You have to have almost a precognition of what's around the next bend. But you need to balance this with an ability to shut out noise, to avoid distraction and to stay focused on what you're doing.

James Dyson: Inventors shouldn't be afraid to take risks. They should embrace failure and learn from their mistakes. I created 5,127 prototypes of the first Dyson bagless vacuum cleaner and only the last one was right! Not being afraid to fail is something I think all successful entrepreneurs have in common. When it comes to leadership, I always wanted to have a team that shared my drive, but also could disagree with me. That was the case when I started with just five people and it is still the case for the five thousand people we now have at Dyson.

Chip Wilson: You need to be there before anyone else. I see so many people open up businesses when the market is far too far along the curve. Let's take snowboarding, for instance –

maybe it starts out with three brands, and within five years you have five hundred competitors and the market eventually consolidates with three companies owning twenty brands each. If you can get in at the beginning, you can be part of the explosive growth journey. What we think of as true entrepreneurs are those who develop ideas that people haven't seen before, but a lot of entrepreneurs can see where we are on the curve and can come in and go, 'Oh, now everyone's going to start going bankrupt because there is so much product, too many competitors and low prices. I'm going to buy up fifty brands, amalgamate them and create a super-brand.' For entrepreneurs with cash, that's a powerful way to do it, but you need a lot of money to make a success of that model. Ultimately, to be an entrepreneur you have to be able to be so driven on getting that idea, that concept you have, up and running, it's just like you can't breathe until you see it come to fruition.

Kiran Mazumdar-Shaw: Entrepreneurship is about very innovative ideas, it's not about copying another successful business. When I think of true entrepreneurship, I think of pioneering spirit. It's where you basically say, 'Hey, I want to do something different, something new, something others have not thought of.' It could be a new idea, a new way of doing things, or a combination of many things. Anyone who imitates or cut-and-pastes a business model is a businessman and *not* an entrepreneur. When I look at something that nobody has thought of, there's a wow factor! When I started Biocon in India, in 1978 when nobody had thought of biotechnology, that was the wow factor. Every time I thought of new technologies or products, I got that same feeling – and that's when I knew I had discovered something that nobody else had.

N. R. Narayana Murthy: The first attribute of an entrepreneur is courage. Great entrepreneurs have courage to dream the impossible, to walk the untrodden paths, to go against the vast majority of naysayers and to make huge sacrifices in the hope that tomorrow will bring better days. The second attribute of an entrepreneur is optimism and hope. When you want to take risks and when you want to walk down the road less travelled or untravelled, you have to be positive and optimistic.

Tory Burch: It comes down to passion. People need to believe in your vision and have confidence in your ability to see it through. There are many great ideas that never materialize. You also have to be willing to embrace risk – calculated risks, because not every risk is worth taking. A great business is always innovating. An entrepreneurial environment is ever-changing and not everyone is suited to this. It's about being flexible and staying calm enough to take it in your stride.

will.i.am: Great entrepreneurs have networks, they have the ability to bring the people together that will help them see their idea through and make it real. There are some people that are really gifted at their craft, for example the best guitarist in the world, or the best pianist in the world, or the best singer in the world, or the best graphic designer, the fastest runner. Just because you're the best at those things doesn't mean you know how to bring people together so that everyone else sees that. Then there's people who network like really, really, really, really amazingly.

How do you separate your identity as an entrepreneur from who you are as an individual?

Sophia Amoruso: I've had multiple identity crises. I remember when I started going up on stage and people used to praise me for my candour. It's like this: I was just too lazy to make things up, honestly. It actually disappoints me when people find candour a novelty. Why is it such a novelty for people to say what they think and how they feel? My question for everyone else is what the fuck is coming out of your mouth? Why am I wasting my time listening to all these people if being honest is the exception, not the rule.

I definitely drank my own Kool-Aid for a while, and I think I became difficult and out of touch. I was hanging out on superyachts in Cannes with billionaires and was considered a 'peer' to people at events like Jeffrey Katzenberg. I was on the *Forbes* 30 under 30, the *Fortune* 40 under 40, the *Inc.* 500, the *Inc.* 30 under 30 and *Vanity Fair*'s New Establishment List. I sat on panels with Brian Chesky and Ben Silverman and was somehow seen as a peer! Or perhaps I was the only girl they could get on stage. It was great to be the token girl at the time; there was nobody else. I became a caricature, and then someone came along and made a Netflix series about me which *really* made me a caricature! This was when the identity crisis really hit me. I was on the cover of *Forbes* in June 2016, my husband left me in July 2016, I fell in love not long after, and my company went bankrupt the day Trump was elected in November 2016. April 2017, a Netflix series about my life that was critically panned came out, and a few months later it was cancelled. A headline from *Vanity Fair* (that had invited me to their Oscars party a year ago) said: 'The most problematic thing about GirlBoss is its source material.' I mean, come on! I take responsibility for everything that happens in my life, but the scale at which it happened, and the ignorance of the people being paid to write headlines about me, was a total mindfuck.

What are the sources of entrepreneurial ideas?

Richard Branson: There are many things that can inspire an entrepreneurial idea – for example, if you receive poor customer service you may be inspired to create a better product or experience. Listen to friends and family – they often have great ideas and can offer invaluable advice. I always carry a small notebook to jot down thoughts, ideas and conversations I have with people when travelling or working. The idea to start an airline came when I was stranded in the Caribbean and decided to charter a flight out – I sold seats to the other stranded passengers to pay for the charter. Have an open mind as you never know when an opportunity or idea might present itself. In the next ten years, we will all head into unknown territory as we face a vast increase in our demand for energy, yet remain worryingly over dependent on oil. If entrepreneurs go into the field of renewable energy for the right reasons, along the way they are likely to create some very exciting new technologies and successful new businesses.

Robin Li: Opportunities generally arise from landscape change. But entrepreneurial ideas can come from anywhere. They can come from recognizing where the pain points, the bottlenecks and the inefficiencies are. They can come from late-night conversations with friends, or from random eureka moments. But for me and for Baidu, one source of entrepreneurial ideas has been the need to serve the under-served population. Serving the under served is a real impetus for innovation. Making technology accessible to people who aren't inherently tech-savvy, and who might be far from fluent with technologies that educated and wealthy urbanites now take for granted, isn't about making simplified, dumbed-down versions. It actually poses technology challenges.

What do you feel are the characteristics of a successful enterprise?

Richard Branson: A great company needs to have an excellent product or service at its core; needs strong management to execute the plan and a good brand to give it the edge over its competitors. It also needs excellent people who really believe in what they're doing. People are at the heart of all Virgin businesses. Often entrepreneurs can create a good product and a brand but need to bring in management to help expand and create a truly great company.

Robin Li: From my own experience, I think success comes from focus and persistence – in my case, focus on and persistence in technology. I've really done one thing for well over twenty years now. I've always believed that hard work and the ability to stick to it can overcome almost any differences in natural intellect among people. Success comes not from IQ but from values, passions, willingness to learn, motivation to improve, and dedication. Focus is not at all easy. There are countless temptations along the way, and often an entrepreneur will waver and be tempted to pivot to another opportunity. For Baidu, in our crucial years, we resisted the siren song of things like wireless value-added services and games, which many of our Chinese peers were seduced by. It may have meant good short-term revenues, but it took them off mission while we continued to stay very focused on search.

N. R. Narayana Murthy: The first attribute of a great business is longevity; that is why I have tremendous respect for companies that have been in business for a long time such as IBM, GE, Unilever and Philips. Commercial longevity is about successfully navigating through peaks and troughs. It's about going through difficult periods, learning to take the inevitable disappointments and continually improve. Longevity is about dusting your knees when you fall down and continuing your journey. It is also the ability to make a difference to society on a sustained basis.

Tony O. Elumelu: I run my businesses according to the principles of Africapitalism, which calls for businesses to commit to development through investing in long-term ventures that increase economic prosperity as well as social wealth. This means that a successful business is one that creates value for its stakeholders but also makes a long-term, sustainable contribution to the communities that it supports and that support it.

⚙⚙

Tony Elumelu's answer here reveals an important difference in the approach to capitalism between nations. In so many fast-growing 'global south' economies, contrary to the narrative we often hear, there is a real commitment from businesses to engage in inclusive growth. Entrepreneurs from these nations aren't necessarily social entrepreneurs in the impact-measured 'double-bottom-line' sense, but are socially minded and aware of their responsibilities to their people. Through my work with the charity In Place of War, I have met entrepreneurs and business owners from across the African continent who have immensely successful and socially engaged companies. In many cases, the realities of war, of social upheaval and of crisis are part of their and their families' histories, so they cannot look away.

What are the most common mistakes entrepreneurs make?

Steve Case: At a macro level, people often don't realize that while having an idea *is* important, executing that idea is more important. There's a Thomas Edison quote I cite a lot which is that 'vision without execution is hallucination'. Having a great idea is *great*, but you have to execute it. There is a tendency to think that the idea itself is a breakthrough, rather than the product, service or business built around the idea. You have to assemble the right team around you, and assemble the right partnerships so that you aren't doing it alone. All too often, this 'go-it-alone' mentality prevails, while partnerships are increasingly important in markets such as health, financial services and education, all of which require a lot of collaborators to create meaningful impact. Entrepreneurs regularly don't fully understand the competitive climate. Often we'll hear people telling us how original their idea is, but our view is that if somebody else isn't doing it, it probably means it isn't a big idea! If something is a good idea, a lot of people will be doing it, and the real question is who will win.

Jerry Yang: Probably the biggest mistake entrepreneurs make is not planning enough for success. Often, when a company is starting out, they are in survival mode. They don't think about what happens when they need to scale (or hyper-scale), or how incumbents might compete once the start-up is on the competitive radar. A misconception about entrepreneurship is that it's a one-person show. But it is nearly impossible for the entrepreneur to do it all; there certainly needs to be a great team behind great entrepreneurs.

Entrepreneurship is an engine of change and progress. We owe much of the comfort of daily life to the success of entrepreneurs who have created millions of jobs and shifted the world forward in the process. From the internet to the automobile, from modern medicine to entertainment, entrepreneurs have been the risk-takers who have seen a better way. In the past quarter-century, entrepreneurs have also applied these same skills to tackling-some of the world's most urgent and pressing problems through philanthropy, social-impact investment and by providing the risk capital needed to spur innovation in the social sector. For those fortunate few entrepreneurs who reach those upper echelons of success, giving back is almost a prerequisite. In the United States, for example, Bill Gates and Warren Buffett launched the Giving Pledge, a movement of entrepreneurs who have committed to give away substantial portions of their wealth in their lifetimes.

What is the role of philanthropy in entrepreneurship?

Richard Branson: I've always regarded business as a powerful tool for delivering positive change in the world, so in my opinion entrepreneurship has a crucial role in addressing these global challenges and many others besides. Public funding and open-ended research are absolutely crucial for coming up with better ideas, novel technology and progressive policy, but it seems only the markets are capable of pouring resources into truly scaling things up; and those markets began with entrepreneurship. Prizes can be a real catalyst for moving an idea along, especially if it's a novel but profoundly important area.

Robin Li: Naturally I support and encourage philanthropy on the part of entrepreneurs, and I'm very glad to see that engagement with broader social issues, giving generously to worthy causes, and working for a common good are now things very much expected of corporations. I would add that the best thing an entrepreneur or company can really do is to build in a real nobility of mission from the very outset. If you set out to do something where your company's success also means bringing tangible benefit to society, that's really the highest form of philanthropy.

Muhammad Yunus: Philanthropy helps address the problems of the people which otherwise remain unaddressed. It is a great concept because this is the only window through which people's problems can be addressed, in a world where businesses are sharply focused on the selfish goal of making profit. But I see a big limitation in philanthropy. Philanthropic money can be used only once. Once it is used the money is gone, it does not come back to the donor. I solved this problem by creating the concept of social business. I make the objectives of philanthropy to be achieved by using the methodology of business, delinking it from the personal profit. This way we get the money back, and we use the same money over and over again and keep on achieving the goal endless times. Philanthropy suddenly becomes very powerful. With this I have brought entrepreneurship and sustainability to philanthropy.

N. R. Narayana Murthy: Entrepreneurship is about the transformation of our world through the power of ideas, and entrepreneurs use the power of their ideas to make this world a better place and, in the process, make money! For many entrepreneurs, they continue this transformational journey through their philanthropy. It is very natural for an entrepreneur to use part of his or her wealth for philanthropy, which, ultimately, is about transforming the world through the power of ideas! Such philanthropic journeys are generally led by social entrepreneurs.

Michael Otto: If we want to change things long term for the better, generous financial donations are not enough. This is why I get personally involved within the framework of my foundation's activities as well as in a range of other socially oriented projects. It is important to me to trigger and drive forward fundamental social, societal and environmental policy initiatives through my own personal involvement. For me, it's not only about 'doing good': alongside the implementation of specific projects I also want to raise people's awareness of particular topics, to seed and nurture ideas and generate momentum that others can then take up and develop further. In my view, projects only make social and societal sense if at some stage they can support and develop themselves.

To what extent are companies having to become communities?

Scott Farquhar: Companies have *always* been communities. Building a community and building a business go hand in hand, that's my belief. Many employees used to check part of themselves at the door when they went to work, and leave part of themselves at home. It could have been because they felt discriminated against, or not accepted, but my view is this: companies that allow employees to bring their whole self to work are the ones that get the most out of their employees. It used to be that work and home were very separate; you left work, went home and didn't really hear from work again till the next day. The lack of the communication systems that we have today left more room for church, for community and all those other things. At the time, people also, for much the same reason, didn't do personal stuff at work. You didn't go to work and update your Facebook page in the middle of the day! Today, work and personal life are bleeding into each other such that the distinction between the two has all but disappeared. If I told my employees they weren't allowed to shop online during their lunchbreak, it would be as weird as telling them to not answer that work email because it's the weekend.

What is the role of failure in the entrepreneurship journey?

Chip Wilson: My goal was to get to the age of fifty and have enough health, and economic success, to survive a downturn. I had a surf, skate, snowboard business for eighteen years which made no money and I wasn't happy with that. I was continuing to take the risk, but it wasn't returning, and eventually the wholesale business was collapsing, it was ceasing to be viable, and I sold it so I could start again. Everything about Lululemon would never have been possible without eighteen years of general failure with West Beach. We have to redefine what failure means. We have to detach it from ego and realize that it's part of our education. My first eighteen years with West Beach were my eighteen-year MBA. Without that, I would not have been able to learn what I needed to, in order to become the world's first fully vertical retail company that went direct to the consumer. There are so many failures and setbacks on the entrepreneurship journey; that's just reality.

Dennis Crowley: Sometimes I don't think people know what they're signing up for when they become entrepreneurs. When you go to the airport and stop at a news-stand, it's wall-to-wall cover stories about successful entrepreneurs, but nobody talks about the failures and very rarely do they talk about the very hard times. Nobody wants to admit that their company almost went out of business ten times. All the talks I give are about failure, how hard it is, how much this job kind of sucks and genuinely how tough it is. People often go into this world thinking it's all roses, and it's not. When people don't talk about this stuff, they think they're the only people to have ever experienced those challenges. The more people talk, the more everyone realizes these are journeys which are shared. Successful entrepreneurs have to speak out about the bad stuff, not just the good. Everyone has a unique path; I truly believe that. You cannot achieve success by replicating someone else's journey, but nevertheless we've all had to fight battles and navigate the success-maze, and with that comes learnings which may help others jump ahead of the curve.

What would be your message to future entrepreneurs?

Robin Li: This is something I speak about quite often, and I always emphasize that entrepreneurs should focus on what they believe is worthwhile, exercising their own judgement without blindly following the crowd. Find that sweet spot at the intersection of what you do best and what you love to do the most, and your odds of success are immediately much higher. If you do what you excel in doing, you'll be better than your competition. And if you focus on what you love to do, you'll be doggedly persistent even when faced with strong competitors, reversals of fortune, and beguiling distractions.

James Dyson: Don't aspire to be an entrepreneur. Aspire to create something that solves a problem. My message to young people with an idea is build a prototype and test it. Test it again and again, making the changes, learning from failure. Don't be afraid to go it alone. Sometimes you have to be brave and jump in at the deep end, but the rewards for creating disruptive technology that really works are truly amazing.

Muhammad Yunus: My message is not to those who are 'interested in entrepreneurship'. They are only a small bunch anyway. My message is to all young people, even if they are not interested at the moment. Every one of them has the potential of turning into great entrepreneurs. My message is a simple question: should you start your life at the top or rather start it at the bottom? If you go for a job, you start at the bottom. There, you'll be busy trying to satisfy your immediate boss, giving up your creative power to fit into a small role defined by your boss. For the rest of your life you'll be dedicated to fulfilling the goals set by your boss, not by you. Have you ever thought of your goals? Why not start with your goals, make your life, and the world, your way. Be the leader, rather than a tiny follower. People will tell you that it is too risky. Don't listen to them. Start by finding your own solutions. The fact that others have not created solutions for you, that's an advantage. You get the chance to try your hand, come up with your ideas. Nobody can beat you on ideas. Try it. There are many like you waiting to join you. Take the first step. I can guarantee you, it is a lot of fun.

José Neves: Continue to innovate and create offers for your market that no one else can. Google is a huge source of inspiration. They've optimized the core business, which is advertising, but they do not give up on funding constant moonshots. One of the greatest lessons I've learned is about culture and values – the culture of a business exists from day one and it really comes from the founder and founding team. Once the company gets bigger, though, you need to verbalize and document the company culture so it is clear to everyone and becomes a mantra. Everything changes when you've hired around a hundred and fifty people, and we now have over three thousand. When we first launched, my job was about finding amazing boutiques, working with the developers to create a product or designing solutions, finding customers. My job now is really about leadership, culture, values and being the ambassador for our business and what we are trying to achieve, as well as of course managing investors. It's a very different job to when I launched Farfetch, but I'm still loving it and am very grateful to the team.

Jamal Edwards: The biggest thing is self-belief. Self-belief is so important. Believe in yourself, try out your ideas. If you fail? Learn from that failure and move on. Don't be harmed by it. Don't let the success get to your head, and don't let the failures get to your heart.

Steve Case: There are still a lot of problems and challenges in society that require fresh thinking, bold perspectives and innovation. The next wave of entrepreneurship could be the most interesting and impactful we've ever seen. There are now entrepreneurs who are focusing on things like how we stay healthy, how we eat, how we get around, how we manage energy, how we learn and many other critically important aspects of the lives of billions. My hope is that entrepreneurs are inspired to take on big challenges. In those challenges are opportunities, and those opportunities could build the next wave of iconic world-changing companies. My hope is that entrepreneurs set their sights high, to tackle big problems and challenges, and take that path of passion and perseverance to have significant impact.

Tony O. Elumelu: I think it is paramount for future entrepreneurs to build sustainable companies that will create value for their stakeholders over the long term. It is also important, however, for these companies to have a social impact. This isn't the easiest path to success, to be sure, but it is responsible and it is my firm belief that this is the foundation upon which great legacies are built.

Jack Welch: Building a great team is what this business game is all about. The team with the best players working together wins. This great team will drive growth, and growth is like an elixir. It's exciting, it creates more and more growth, and it's a helluva lot of fun. Business is fun, it's a game. You're playing against others, and you want to win. Winning is good, losing is bad! Do you want to be in the winner's locker room celebrating or in the loser's with your head down and a towel around your neck? If you're winning, you can give back – to your family, institutions of your choice, and your local communities. If you're losing, your pockets are empty.

Naveen Jain: You have to dream so big that people think you're crazy. If people don't think you're crazy, you're not dreaming big enough. You can never be afraid of failing. As an entrepreneur, you never fail – you adapt and pivot. Ideas fail, people don't. If you are smart enough to adapt and pivot, you realize that ideas are stepping stones.

will.i.am: You have to figure out who you are in the conversation. You have to know who you are at the table. Are you the idea guy? The notetaker? The make-it-happen guy? The follow-through guy? Or the bring-it-together person? In a proper thinking session, you have those personalities. The idea guy, the guru (who brings people together, not necessarily the same person as the idea guy), the notetaker (who takes everything down and collates it), the make-it-happen guy (who creates the action points, and understands what needs to be done) and the follow-through guy (who makes those actions happen). There's also an 'assembler' who knows how to bring all these people together. Are you that person? Who are you? I'm an ideas person. I know exactly that's who I am. I'm not a good follow-through guy, I sometimes overthink things too much and I can be overprotective of my ideas. As an ideas person and a facilitator you will want to get your idea out when you think it's finished, and that's often suffocating for your business because you don't allow it to grow.

Kevin O'Leary: The first thing you need is to get your finances in order. I tell all my students the same thing. If anything's been learned on the lessons of a decade of *Shark Tank*, and *Dragon's Den* in England and Canada and Australia, the format's the same in all the countries. These three elements are found in all successful pitches. First, you have to get in front of those sharks or dragons, and explain in ninety seconds or less what the opportunity is. If you can't do that, you're going to fail. Second, you have to explain why you're the right person to execute the business plan. What do you know? What makes you unique? What has your experience been? Why are you the right person? A great idea with a bad execution is a horrible investment, so you have to prove to me you can actually execute. Lastly, and this is the one that I take personal pride in, if you don't know your numbers, I will make sure you burn in hell in perpetuity. You have to know your numbers. If you're going to get in front of me and talk about a business, you'd better know the break-even analysis, the gross margin, size of the market, number of competitors. All of that stuff. I expect you to know that; that's just a given. If you don't, you're going to fail.

Stewart Butterfield: First, you have to put the customer ahead of yourself. Second, I cannot overstate the importance of aligning and committing to a vision, and not constantly second-guessing yourself. There's absolutely important feedback that comes from having your product in market, but it's far too easy to be swayed by that and hesitate or change course. For a company like Slack, with our kind of growth, it feels a little bit like parkour. You're moving very quickly, opportunistically trying to take advantage of things in your environment. In parkour that might be walls or railings, but for us it's changes in the market or what our customers need. The consequences are similar: if you hesitate, you're going to crash and probably hurt yourself. It's better to be slightly off in a decision but moving full speed ahead than to let doubt stop you.

⚙️⚙️

At the beginning of this chapter, I admitted that I didn't know what an entrepreneur was until I was called one. Today, the most visible part of entrepreneurship has become a Hollywood caricature of itself – productized into books, seminars and consultancies led by entrepreneurship influencers who make more money from their social followings than from actual businesses. I think it's important that we disconnect that from reality.

Across the world there are people who are driven to look for solutions to problems, who have a passion that turns into a business, who want to change the world, who have a drive to create or who have no choice but to start a business to make their way in life. Whether it's the local store owner, or someone who founded a global business, entrepreneurs are everywhere and form the backbone to our economy. The thread that connects all of them, however, is the ability to turn an idea into a reality, and the tenacity to see that through, a characteristic

Sir James Dyson described to me when he talked about how important it was that entrepreneurs had the traits of drive and commitment to see their ideas through to fruition.

In much the same way as its biological counterpart, entrepreneurial evolution is a story of the success of good ideas. Billions of iterations occur, and those that add value to the system of humanity flourish, becoming part of our culture with increasing rapidity. The Wright brothers made the first powered flight in 1903 over a distance of 120 feet – just sixty-six years later, two humans stood on the moon looking back at earth. In a similar feat, our species progressed in less than seventy years from the first basic digital computer in 1941 to having the total sum of human knowledge in a globally connected amorphous cloud of computers.

The early days of the internet era were some of the most exciting in entrepreneurship. Small groups of people created global businesses at a scale never before seen, and with that came learnings on entrepreneurship in a very extreme environment. Jerry Yang was the co-founder of Yahoo!, one of the first search engines, and the company made him one of the world's first internet billionaires. As we've heard in this chapter, entrepreneurship for him was about finding a common, strong mission to build something that would change the world. And to do that you need a team that shares that passion and belief, the success and failure, together. Without exception, every one of the most successful entrepreneurs I've ever met is aligned with this view.

Our innate capability to generate ideas is potentially the most powerful faculty we have at our disposal. Entrepreneurs are simply the people who take a gamut of resources – capital, knowledge, tools, infrastructure – and transform their ideas into physical or virtual assets, which can then be absorbed into society and wider culture. Put in its most simple terms by Buddha, 'We are what we think. All that we are arises with our thoughts. With our thoughts, we make the world.'

BIOGRAPHIES

Sophia Amoruso is an American businesswoman and the founder of Girlboss Media, a professional network for ambitious women. Her bestselling autobiography #*GIRLBOSS* was adapted into a scripted TV series for Netflix.

Steve Ballmer is a businessman and investor, and was the Chief Executive Officer of Microsoft from 2000 to 2014. He is also the current owner of the Los Angeles Clippers.

Sir Richard Branson is a British entrepreneur, investor and author. He is the founder of Virgin, which controls more than 400 companies in various fields.

Tory Burch is an American fashion designer, businesswoman and philanthropist. She is Executive Chairman and Chief Creative Officer of the fashion label Tory Burch.

Stewart Butterfield is a Canadian entrepreneur and businessman. He is the co-founder of photo-sharing website Flickr and co-founder and CEO of Slack.

Steve Case is an American entrepreneur, investor and businessman. He is the former CEO and chairman of AOL and is known for his advocacy for immigration reform.

Dennis Crowley is an internet entrepreneur. He is the co-founder of Foursquare and Dodgeball, and founder of the semi-professional soccer team Kingston Stockade FC in New York.

Sir James Dyson CBE is an award-winning British inventor and entrepreneur, and the founder of Dyson. He is well known for his work on revolutionizing vacuum cleaners and has won many design awards for his appliances.

Jamal Edwards MBE is a British entrepreneur, model, bestselling author and the founder of the online music platform SB.TV and the London-based youth centre project, Jamal Edwards Delve.

Tony O. Elumelu is a Nigerian economist, entrepreneur and philanthropist, and Chairman of Heirs Holdings, United Bank for Africa, Transcorp and founder of the Tony Elumelu Foundation.

Scott Farquhar is an Australian entrepreneur. He is the co-founder and CEO of enterprise software company Atlassian, whose clients include NASA, Tesla and SpaceX.

Naveen Jain is a business executive, entrepreneur and the founder and former CEO of InfoSpace, co-founder and Executive Chairman of Moon Express and founder and CEO of Viome.

Donna Karan is an American fashion designer and the founder of the Donna Karan New York and DKNY clothing labels. In 2007, she began her lifestyle brand, Urban Zen.

Robin Li is a Chinese software engineer and entrepreneur. He is the co-founder of the search engine Baidu, the fifth most popular website in the world after Google, YouTube, Tmall and Facebook.

Kiran Mazumdar-Shaw is an Indian entrepreneur. She is the Chairperson and Managing Director of the biotechnology company Biocon Limited and the former Chairperson of the Indian Institute of Management. In 2019, she was listed as sixty-fifth on the *Forbes* list of 'Most Powerful Women in the World'.

N. R. Narayana Murthy is an Indian software entrepreneur and co-founder of tech giant Infosys. He has been named one of the twelve greatest entrepreneurs of our time by Fortune magazine.

José Neves is a Portuguese businessman and the founder of the global luxury fashion platform, Farfetch.

Kevin O'Leary is a businessman, author, politician and television personality. Since 2009, he has been a fixture on the business reality TV show *Shark Tank*.

Professor Michael Otto is a German entrepreneur. He is the head of the mail order company, Otto Group, which is second only to Amazon.com as a web retailer.

Gary Vaynerchuk is a Belarusian-American entrepreneur and bestselling author. He is the co-founder of Resy and Empathy Wines, Chairman of VaynerX and CEO of VaynerMedia.

Jack Welch (1935–2020) was an American business executive, chemical engineer and bestselling author. He was Chairman and CEO of General Electric between 1981 and 2001.

will.i.am is an American rapper, singer, songwriter, producer and actor. He is a member of the Black Eyed Peas and is also known for his appearances as a judge on *The Voice*.

Chip Wilson is a businessman and philanthropist, and the founder of Lululemon Athletica, widely credited as being behind the 'athleisure' trend.

Jerry Yang is an entrepreneur and computer programmer, co-founder and former CEO of Yahoo! Inc. and founder of AME Cloud Ventures.

Professor Muhammad Yunus is a social entrepreneur, banker and economist. He has been awarded many prizes for his work, including the Nobel Peace Prize in 2006 for founding the Grameen Bank in Bangladesh and launching the revolutionary concepts of microcredit and microfinance.

5

ON DISCRIMINATION AND INJUSTICE: THEM AND US

'We have to put ourselves into the shoes of the other and not adhere to the cult of ignorance.'

ROSE McGOWAN

I was only a child when my mum and dad took me to ride the Space Tower at Blackpool Pleasure Beach, an amusement park in the north of England. This forty-eight-metre-high rotating observation deck gave a panoramic view of all the attractions and seemed to be a great way to start the visit. I remember feeling hugely excited, in the giddy way you do as a child. But this excitement quickly evaporated as the father of another family on the ride at the same time as us proceeded to launch into a tirade of statements, including, but not limited to, 'Why don't you fuck off back to your own country, you Pakis!' This was my earliest experience of racism, although I didn't know what it was at the time. For my parents, who came to Britain in the 1960s, racism was an ever-present part of their early lives in the UK. To give you just a couple of examples, when my father first came to Manchester, he lived in a one-room bedsit, which cost him £5 a week. He was looking around for a better place to live and found a nice flat in the popular area of Didsbury. He rang the landlord immediately to go and look around, but when he got there, as soon as she opened the door, she paused, took a breath, and said, 'Sorry, it's already gone.' This was not an isolated incident. For my dad, hearing people shouting 'Paki! Go home!' was a regular thing. I asked my dad how he got past this, and he told me that he just assumed it was a fact of life in the UK. He saw the warmth of some people's welcome in the business community in particular, and so tried to overlook it. For many communities who came to Britain at a similar time as my parents, the response was fight or flight. Fight meaning integration, and flight resulting in building insular communities. The former was the more successful option, but a phenomenon that did require both sides to be open to the idea.

Growing up in the 1980s, racism was a part of my life. From being called 'curry pot' and 'paki' at school, to the fortunately rarer incidents of on-street racism, I took it for granted that there were a lot of people who simply didn't like me because I was brown. While I wasn't pleased about this, it felt like a social norm, part of how society worked at the time. Thankfully, as we moved into the 1990s and 2000s, racism became less of an issue for me. Some of this was due to my migration into the nice leftie middle-class bubble my career allowed me to enter, but I think a lot was genuinely due to racism slowly becoming significantly less acceptable in our society. I mostly felt blissfully unaware of my skin culture unless it was specifically pointed out, such as on one occasion early in my business career when a journalist asked me, 'So, Vikas, how does it feel to be an Asian entrepreneur?', a question to which my answer was simple: 'I guess like any other entrepreneur, but brown?' This may seem a fairly harmless exchange, but sometimes the 'them and us' in society only becomes apparent when pointed out. Over the past few years, however, I've realized that the racism I experienced in my youth is just as strong – it was just pushed a little deeper into the shadows.

For the first time in over twenty years, I feel brown. I find myself being extra careful in terms of how I dress, where I go, how I speak, what I carry and how I behave – not to conform to any new social norms, but rather so that people don't mistake me for a terrorist, or make assumptions about my intentions. I am not the only brown person I know who has a 'pre-flight shave' at airports, nor the only one I know who is acutely aware of themselves on public transport.

Discrimination isn't just a race issue. Around the world, people are economically, socially and culturally marginalized (and often face violence and displacement) because of their gender, skin colour, socio-economic background, religion, sexuality and political affiliation. You need only look to the United States to see the awful reality of systemic, institutionalized racism that has cost the lives of so many African Americans at the hands of systems that are ostensibly there to protect them. And the global protests following the murder of George Floyd in May 2020 made it very clear that for many, enough is enough – and things have to change.

In this chapter are some of my conversations with leaders and activists who have dedicated their careers to exposing and fighting discrimination in all its forms – F. W. de Klerk, former president of South Africa, who talked to me about apartheid, Holocaust survivor Iby Knill, who shared with me her experiences during the Second World War, and actor George Takei, who spoke about his own experiences being a prisoner at a US internment camp. Activist Ai Weiwei spoke to me about arts and activism and actor Rose McGowan about her experience of gender discrimination, while Sir Philip Craven, former president of the International Paralympic Committee, talked about the discrimination facing those with disabilities. Nobel Peace Prize-winner Leymah Gbowee shared her views with me on the struggle for gender rights, alongside Melinda Gates who spoke of the solutions to gender-based discrimination. Ruth Hunt and Peter Tatchell discussed the challenges faced by LGBT+ communities, and the late Harry Leslie Smith and the Right Honourable Lord Bird addressed the challenges facing those in society who are impacted by poverty and economic marginalization. I also spoke to comedian and author David Baddiel about the role played by the internet in our experience of discrimination, and how it manifests in the digital world.

How has poverty changed in your lifetime?

Harry Leslie Smith: Poverty has changed a lot in my lifetime, though there are certain similarities and echoes which have always carried through. The poverty I experienced in my youth during the 1920s and 1930s was much more extreme than most hard-pressed people will endure today. We lived in appalling conditions – in doss houses in a rough neighbourhood of Bradford. There was no welfare state, homelessness was rife, and the poor lived in a libertarian dystopia where assistance was minimal, and misery was all encompassing. There was no National Health Service, which meant that if you couldn't afford healthcare, you died sooner, and generally with a greater degree of anguish, than someone in the middle or upper classes. Poverty today is all around us. Although it may not be as extreme as the 1930s, I fear it is heading that way because of many years of austerity, which has gutted the welfare state. I am starting to see a similar type of meanness towards low-income workers and the poor that I witnessed during the Great Depression. There is a feeling today, like in my youth, that this will not end. It's my responsibility, as an eyewitness to history, to tell people the anguish of poverty can be eradicated, but only through action and political change – and that starts with voter registration. We have to get people out to vote more.

What is the role of government in the eradication of poverty?

Lord John Bird: To understand poverty, you have to understand the role government money has played. Our taxes have been invested into social security mechanisms which, at best, have become a form of hand holding. Social security, when it was first invented, was there to help people through a tough time and to move them on to success through training and provision. That was social opportunity hidden within social security legislation. In today's world, social security warehouses people and because it's warehoused people for so long, when the government tries to make changes, they've already sowed the seeds for their own destruction. They've harmed the normal acquisition of skills people need to provide for themselves, their families and their children. Government has destroyed the impetus for people to become entrepreneurs, and to build skills.

People still see 'the poor' as another species. If you scrape the surface of most white middle-class liberals in the UK who are doing quite well out of society, you will find, some generations ago, there was an individual who sowed the seeds of getting that family out of poverty. It may have been a grandfather who learned a new skill, or who was committed to start a business. A generation later, that entire family no longer had to know about poverty.

For over ten years, I've worked closely with Mustard Tree, a charity in Manchester that supports thousands of individuals across the region who are impacted by poverty and marginalization. In the United Kingdom, we're lucky to have a reasonable social safety net, but even that is like a thumb being held over a crack in a dam, as the pressure builds behind it. Like so many governments across the world, ours in the United Kingdom has prioritized wealth creation at a huge cost. Housing is unaffordable, jobs have moved to the services and financial sector, communities and safety nets have been underfunded, and the net result is a set of conditions that puts millions of lives in a precarious state. We are one of the richest countries in the world, but research (from the Joseph Rowntree Foundation) shows that the UK has a poverty rate of 22 per cent (that's around 14 million people, one in five of our population) and 1.5 million of those have experienced destitution (including over 300,000 children). During the Covid lockdowns of 2020, at Mustard Tree we experienced demand levels that were off the charts, as families who had been just about getting by suddenly found themselves unable to cope.

⚙⚙

What is the true scale of discrimination faced by people living with impairments and disabilities?

Philip Craven: I personally don't encounter any discrimination that often, but I wouldn't go to places or meet with people again if they gave me that impression. That said, I'm sure that much discrimination exists. The real way to change perceptions in society against these mythical 'groups' of people is through positive experiences, and not to just ram new laws down their throats. In some cases, however, these laws are necessary. Wider parking spaces, for example, mean that people can get out of their chair into the front seat of their cars. Education is imperative in all formats to do this, as it allows people themselves to change their minds about others rather than being told they have to believe or act in a certain way. Around ten years ago in the USA, Paralympians were called 'super-crips' by some people in the communities they themselves were supposed to belong to, perhaps because people couldn't associate with them. But in truth, they are there to showcase what is possible when you really put your mind to it. You only change perceptions by showing yourself as being what you are. People won't do it for you.

What does the term 'disability' really mean?

Philip Craven: The word disability is the embodiment of pure negativity and when it's used as a catch-all such as 'the disabled' it's even worse. Everyone is an individual, and those individual personalities should shine through, not the labels. Ask a person who's getting a bit older and may have a visual, hearing or mobility impairment, if they're disabled? They'll throw that title off vehemently! They view disability as being a community they don't belong to. I'm Philip Craven, I'm me. The fact that I use a wheelchair is immaterial. I am what I am.

At the 2010 Winter Olympics in Vancouver, we were staying at the Westin. They had an adapted bathroom, with a little sink that never emptied. I called one of the hotel team, who pointed out the sink was on a siphon, and that siphon had to be half filled with whatever you had spat out into the sink before it emptied. I told the hotel it wasn't acceptable to have something this crude in a five-star hotel, and the response was, well, what do you expect, it's a disabled sink in a disabled bathroom. This clearly illustrates the way people think, assuming we want something different when we don't. If you're told you're disabled long enough, you start to feel it. I sometimes get asked if things changed for me after my accident. They didn't because I damn well made sure they didn't and fought against it. You have to throw off your impairments and make sure that you have the confidence to decide your own destiny rather than allowing others to decide it for you because you're disabled.

What would be your message to those living with disabilities?

Philip Craven: You have to be yourself and decide what you want to do with your life. If you have negative thoughts at the moment, you have to see what other people have done in your situation, but realize it's you that will change your life with the support of others, not others that will change your life for you. You have to get information in your mind about what's possible, but you need determination to go and get it, and if anyone stands in your way, fight them like mad. Life's a fight, it's a struggle, and you have to take it to them. You are in a community with written and unwritten rules, but life is for freedom. You have to create your own freedom.

In 2019, with one of the charities I support, In Place of War, I went to visit communities in the north of Uganda, not far from the border with South Sudan, that had been impacted by decades of violent conflict. We were creating a series of programmes there to address the inequalities facing those with disabilities; in this case predominantly as a result of landmines. Using interactive drama workshops based around the 'forum theatre' technique, we discovered that it wasn't specifically a bias against disability that was causing the manifest discrimination, but rather that, since the end of the war, hospitals had been built, meaning that individuals who had come into contact with landmines now survived with disabilities, rather than dying due to a lack of medical treatment. The communities we visited simply did not understand disability, nor did they have the language to discuss it. Being able to have that conversation moved the needle dramatically, even in the short time we were with them. And that's true of so many forms of discrimination; unless we keep having conversations, we risk going backwards.

Right at the start of this chapter, I highlighted my own experience of racism. It takes only a cursory glance at the news to realize that the growth of right-wing populist and nationalist movements around the world in the past decade has brought racial discrimination back to the forefront. Our world has fought hard against this, and unfortunately it seems we must continue to do so.

What is race?

Dexter Dias QC: As a biological, scientific, genetic concept, race does not exist. The truth is we are a relatively new species and we are all just African migrants with different migratory patterns and trajectories. I find comfort in that thought about our shared humanity. But here's the thing: if race doesn't exist, and is in fact a social construct, a myth that has been meticulously assembled, why has it become one of the most important forces on the entire planet? The reason is the function myths perform. We tell each other stories to achieve purposes, to create meaning in the world, to inform and justify actions, to organize our societies – and ourselves.

The myth of race started to take off around the time of the Spanish Inquisition, just over five hundred years ago when the Spanish tried to establish that Jewish people were a different species, not the same as them. The idea of race really went viral, however, because of colonialism – a project that fundamentally depended on using the production of 'race' as a form of knowledge to justify the exploitation of people in other lands which were being appropriated and asset-stripped. By recasting them through the lens of spurious pseudoscience as inferior, somehow not human in the same way, a lot of the work of domination was done. The concept of racial difference is almost always a direct function of some form of exploitation, rubber-stamped under the banner of 'race'. Race is very versatile. I always remember what the sociologist Pierre Bourdieu says: 'There is not racism; there are racisms' – plural. That idea is very important in understanding what is happening in the world right now.

What is the relationship between race and identity?

Afua Hirsch: We take for granted the fact that we have racial identities that don't coincide with anything real in the sense of biology or science. There are no genes that correlate to our notion of race. In fact, there are greater genetic differences within ethnic groups than between them. It's easy to trace the history of how we came to see ourselves in such racialized ways. Race is an idea that was invented very specifically as an ideology to exploit people and land around the world, as the Europeans did during the period of imperialist expansion. As Ta-Nehisi Coates said, 'Race is not the child of slavery, slavery is the child of race.' To be clear, it was not just the Europeans who embarked on colonialism, but the European model of it was rooted in the ideological foundations of race and racial categorization, tools that served to justify the degradation of Africans to the extent that they were no longer regarded as human. The ways in which those ideas about race were socially constructed have endured and the evidence shows that they become internalized to the point where we self-identify through the lens of race. We need to continue to interrogate the reasons why we, as a society, have been racialized and the ideological content of that racialization.

In your view, what caused the racial segregation during colonial times that culminated in apartheid?

F. W. de Klerk: The concept of human rights is a fairly new phenomenon in human affairs. For most of history, even among the indigenous peoples of Africa, America and Asia, it was accepted that conquering powers could treat vanquished peoples and their territories more or less as they wanted. The behaviour of colonial powers towards the people they conquered was seldom restrained by law, morality or compassion, particularly in the Americas. Relationships between settlers and the indigenous population in South Africa were generally less exploitive and less repressive than they were in the Americas, Australasia and in many parts of Asia. Most colonial powers practised segregation against the peoples they conquered for a number of reasons: they believed that their status as Christians gave them a right to discriminate against pagans; there were often substantial differences in levels of development between the colonial powers and the people they subjugated; colonizers were often ignorant about the cultures that they encountered; they were usually motivated by determination to seize the land and the resources of colonial peoples; and they had an interest in keeping colonial peoples in a state of subjugation to prevent them from rising in rebellion. However, for much of their history, a majority of black South Africans continued to live in their own tribal areas where they were ruled by their traditional authorities (whose appointment was, however, approved by white governments in Pretoria).

In South Africa's case, segregation had its roots in a strong view that each of the peoples of the region should be encouraged to develop separately. From the late 1950s onwards, South Africa embarked on a policy of internal decolonization that culminated in the development of ten homelands, each with its own parliament, government, administration – and often its own university. Almost 40 per cent of black South Africans lived in these areas and were, for all practical purposes, governed by their own people without any kind of racial discrimination. Six of the territories progressed to the stage of self-government and four were granted full independence that was recognized only by South Africa and each other. Nevertheless, most of the states had budgets and economies larger than those of quite a number of independent countries elsewhere in Africa. The policy failed because the territories set aside for blacks were too small and fragmented; because economic forces were drawing more and more black people into the so-called white economy; because the policy made no provision for the political rights of black people in the so-called white areas where whites were also a minority; and because the policy was vehemently rejected by a great majority of non-white South Africans.

What led to the abolition of apartheid?

F. W. de Klerk: There were a number of factors that led to the abolition of apartheid. Firstly, the clear failure of the government's policy to achieve a just solution to the problems of the country; the rejection of apartheid by the overwhelming majority of non-white South Africans leading to a spiral of resistance and repression; growing international isolation and sanctions; increasing integration of black South Africans into the economy leading to substantial shifts in the distribution of income; emergence of the majority of Afrikaners into the middle class, with university education and increasing exposure to international attitudes; the acceptance by the end of the 1980s that there was no prospect for either a military or a revolutionary solution; the successful implementation of the UN independence process in Namibia following the negotiated withdrawal of Cuban troops from Namibia; the emergence of a new generation of National Party leaders after the stroke suffered by President P. W. Botha at the beginning of 1989; the positive influence of exploratory talks between white business and academic leadership groups and the ANC – parallel to the initiation of informal talks between Nelson Mandela and the SA government; and the collapse of the Soviet Union and the victory of free-market democracy.

Why are institutions slow or reluctant to respond to racism?

Afua Hirsch: We're talking here about deeply entrenched structural inequalities that benefit the elite. It will take profound changes in our society to remedy those inequalities, and so most diversity and inclusion strategies focus on identities such as gender and sexual orientation, identities which have certainly been a source of structural inequalities, but have certainly not resulted in the level of inequality that race has when you look at distribution of outcomes in society. The hypocrisy of modern corporations can be seen in how they claim to represent certain values, but really continue to represent elitism and the concentration of power and wealth among a few, who can often trace their actual descent to people who benefited from colonial slavery. It's so much easier to talk about diversity; it's a catch-all that allows you to have people who look different in the room without acknowledging whiteness and how racism was constructed and continues to work. We always find ways of taking the safe route; even when we talk of racism, we lump it into a 'BAME issue', which is alien to real, lived experience.

How do media portrayals of race impact on racism?

George Takei: I'm an actor, and I know the power of the media, its stereotypes and its power to shape people's attitudes towards groups of people. When Pearl Harbor happened, we had an Attorney General in California, a great man who knew the law and the constitution. He was the top lawyer in the State of California, wanted to become governor and saw that the top issue in California at the time was to lock up the Japanese movement and the Japanese people. This man, who knew better, got up and made an amazing statement as Attorney General. He said, 'We have no reports of spying or sabotage or fifth column activities by Japanese Americans, and that is ominous. The Japanese are inscrutable, and it would be prudent to lock them up before they do anything.' Just think about that. This is an Attorney General who used the absence of evidence, as evidence.

He became enormously powerful as the leader of the internment movement in California. He fed into the wartime hysteria, which travelled right up to the President of the United States. It was President Roosevelt who signed the Executive Order that put us into these barbed-wire camps. This Attorney General ran for governor, won, held two terms in office and was then appointed as the Chief Justice of the Supreme Court of the United States. You might recognize his name: Earl Warren, the so-called liberal Chief Justice of the United States. I like to think he was liberal because of his conscience; he never owned up to the role he played in California as Attorney General, but in his posthumous memoirs he wrote that his greatest regret was the role he played in the internment of Japanese Americans. But this was not something he was prepared to say while he was alive.

○◎○

The Holocaust is recent history. Within the lifetimes of people who are still alive today, the world witnessed the systematic execution of over 6 million people because of their religion. Since this abhorrent act, we have seen genocide and ethnic cleansing take place around the world as predominantly authoritarian leaders divide and dehumanize people along racial and cultural lines. Throughout the twentieth century we have heard the survivors of atrocities speak to the world and say 'never again' – and we owe it to them, and to ourselves, to listen.

Did your experiences at Auschwitz change your sense of identity?

Iby Knill: Initially, after the liberation, everyone felt survivors' guilt. Why did we survive when others didn't? What do we now have to do in order to earn and deserve the fact that we were still alive? This is common with survivors, and colours the way you look at life and your own actions. You evaluate things on that basis and you try to be a better person. You try not to harm people, and try not to damage or belittle others because you have experienced yourself what it is to be belittled.

I had a nervous breakdown for the first three years. Had it not been for a very understanding husband, I don't think I would have survived. My late husband had been a soldier in the First World War and experienced trench warfare. He understood the trauma of what I was going through. It took several more years to get some form of balanced mental state. I wrapped up those memories into a Pandora's box, threw it in the sea and threw away the key. I would never talk about it or refer to it, nor would my mother, who had also been in a camp. We would never mention to each other anything about it. You pretended that period of time never existed. During my time in Auschwitz, it was impossible to isolate good from bad and so that period disappeared. To the extent that for those years afterwards, I could not speak German, which had previously been my main language. It is only now, since 2002 when I started my book, that I concluded it was time to put down what I had experienced and bear witness to it.

What was the importance of sharing the stories of Auschwitz, and what can society learn from your experiences?

Iby Knill: It's very important for people to realize that you mustn't allow a culture of us and them to develop. When you look at young people, they play together regardless of their colour or background. Somewhere along the line they start to feel that other people are different to them. I'm not saying we should all revert to childlike innocence, but rather that this feeling of equality should remain, that we feel that under the skin we are all the same. I find it very important to talk to young people about it, and make them aware of what the end result of a culture of dehumanization can be. I spend a lot of time talking to young people about the fact that our differences only make life more interesting, and more valuable. It would be very dull if we were all the same.

It's sobering to realize that more girls have been killed in the past fifty years simply because of their gender than all the men in all the battles of the twentieth century. Even today, more than 3 million women around the world are enslaved in the sex trade, with millions more facing economic, social and cultural injustice simply because of their gender. The Rome Statute, which created the International Criminal Court, defines crimes against humanity as part of 'a wide practice of atrocities tolerated or condoned by a government or a de-facto authority' – and it is against this definition that we begin to see that women are facing, and have suffered, one of the greatest human rights atrocities of this century. The past few years has seen the systemic and institutionalized sexism in society laid bare for the world to see; and one of the most powerful examples of this has been the exposing of sexual abuse and sexism within the media through the #MeToo movement. Rose McGowan has been a visible and powerful voice in this movement, and I wanted to speak to her and others about their experiences, and why it's so important to speak about this now.

Why do we still need to have conversations around sexism?

Rose McGowan: People have been shamed for coming forward for such a long time that we still need to have these conversations again and again. These conversations are ugly, nobody wants to have them – let's put that out there. It's not a walk in the park to come forward, it's not fun, but growth is ugly and sometimes growth hurts. That's the point in time we're at now. Sexism has always been 'tolerated'. The way I get treated in the media every day is wildly sexist, and I can go on Twitter at any time and just be flooded by sexist and nasty messages. So many people think or say, 'I'm one of the good guys', or 'I'm one of the good women', and I just say to them, be better. I'm no expert on race, but I can say that since I was fourteen, I can remember story after story of black people getting shot in America, and nothing has changed – we're still talking about it, but people still aren't being held accountable. We're living at a time where people are being assassinated because of their colour, in a society that has been programmed to be fearful of different races. We need to unlearn what we've learned, and replace that with knowledge of other races, through their eyes, their writers, their media. We have to put ourselves into the shoes of the other and not adhere to the cult of ignorance.

What does feminism mean to you?

Laura Bates: Everybody deserves to be treated equally, regardless of their sex. Very simply and clearly, that's what feminism means to me. Believing that women have the right to economic, social and political equality to men is the basis of feminism – and if you apply that definition, I hope very few people would be able to say they are not feminists.

I came to feminism firstly through personal experiences of inequality, sexual violence and harassment. In 2012, I had a group of such experiences in a relatively short space of time and that prompted me to talk to other women and girls and ask them if they'd experienced these things too. I was completely overwhelmed by the responses. I thought that perhaps one or two women would have an experience to share from some point in their lives, but every single woman I spoke to shared experiences that happened to them every single day. Women told me about experiences they'd had on the way to meet me that day, or how in their workplace, male colleagues would take clients to a strip club at lunchtime and missed out on deals. They told me how they were followed in the street, licked, touched, harassed, abused, you name it. The severity and universality of sexism shocked me. It made me realize how little awareness there was around it. The majority of women I spoke to told me that until I asked them outright about their experiences, they had never told anyone. Why? They thought it was just normal life and didn't want to make a fuss. Sexism is a major problem, affecting women's lives on a daily basis.

What is the scale and reality of sexism faced by women?

Laura Bates: Sexism is a huge, severe problem. We've received over one hundred thousand testimonies from women all over the world, and find there are certain themes which come up over and over again.

In the UK, when women try to speak out against gender inequality we're often told, 'You don't know how lucky you are! Look at what women are dealing with elsewhere!' But here's the thing: in the UK every year, 54,000 women lose their jobs as a result of paternity discrimination, 85,000 women are raped and 400,000 sexually assaulted. The idea that women simply aren't facing these severe issues in the UK is false. The issues women face are complex and interconnected. If we look at the objectification of women in the media or the harassment of women in the street, we see the same words and slurs used that may be directed at a woman facing discrimination in a meeting, or at the victim of domestic abuse. To write off and excuse certain elements of sexism and misogyny is simply wrong, especially when we live in a world with an epidemic of violence, abuse and inequality against women. Sexism is not a women's issue, it's a human rights issue. This is not about vilifying men, or victimizing women – it's about people standing up to prejudice.

Why does so much of our culture reduce the value of women to their appearance?

Jameela Jamil: I don't think there's ever been a time where women haven't been reduced to being much more than sex objects or carriers for children; we've rarely been seen with much more value than our appeal to men. What surprises me so much about the fact that these attitudes still prevail is that we had a moment in the 1990s where I felt change was really coming, and women were stepping into power, into different boxes, and out of the pigeon holes that we were pushed back into. This was the era just before heroin chic, where we had Lauryn Hill, Missy Elliott and so many new stories being told. We had female directors like Sofia Coppola rising through the ranks, and it felt like there was a real turning point where women were being very openly intellectual, bold and varied.

After this, it's felt like the plot has been dialled back; maybe because we were making too much progress, and the patriarchy didn't like it. Today, with the help of social media, we're seeing the most aggressive assault on our appearance that there has ever been.

How is social media impacting on people's image of themselves?

Jameela Jamil: The statistics show that we're seeing the highest rates of teen surgery, self-harm and eating disorders that we've ever experienced. Women are under a visceral attack. When I was younger, you at least had to go out and find a toxic magazine, or ask someone for the £4 to buy it. Or look very hard for the hidden thinspiration accounts. You would have to actively seek out the kind of content that is now thrust in your face. Now, because of algorithms, and because we're all complicit in pushing out this narrative of being thin and flawless, using filters and all that madness, it is the first thing we see when we open our phones in bed. Especially if you're a woman, you are algorithmically attacked with imagery of women who make you feel bad about yourself, about your life and your looks. Teenagers literally can't get away from it. As a young woman, if you want to take part in social media, you will see these crazy adverts for corsets, appetite suppressants, and so much more – whether you are looking for them or not.

Celebrities are so toxic, as is this influencer culture which has emerged. Ninety-five per cent of celebrities are complicit in the assault on women by not saying anything about it, by not calling out the use of Photoshop, and actually by perpetuating the narrative that looks are the most important thing by only ever talking about looks, and having surgeries without admitting it. Let me be clear, I don't mind whether someone wants to have surgery or not, but if you have and you don't admit it, you're committing a crime against your gender.

How have your own life experiences shaped how you approach tackling the issues faced by women and girls internationally?

Melinda Gates: One example is family planning. When I started travelling for our foundation, I began meeting women who told me they had no access to contraceptives and because of that, no voice in their families or their futures. They were having more children than they could afford to feed, and they were getting pregnant too often for their bodies to handle. Their stories got me thinking about what contraceptives have meant in my own life. Because the truth is that they've meant everything. My family, my career and my life as I know it are all a direct result of the fact that I could and did use contraceptives. Bill and I waited to start having kids until we were ready. And we waited three years between each kid, because that's what was right for our family. If you live in the US or Europe, it can be easy to take these options for granted. But there are more than 200 million women around the world who don't want to get pregnant but don't have access to modern contraceptives. I never expected that I was going to become an advocate for contraceptives, and I never, ever thought I'd be speaking publicly about my own experience with them, but I couldn't turn my back on the women I met.

Why do you think women suffer so much injustice around the world?

Leymah Gbowee: It's because of the way the world is shaped. We've never had an equal dynamic. If you go back, for those of us who call ourselves Christians, the sin of the world is blamed on women. Eve was the one who turned a perfect world imperfect. If you are the one taking the world from perfection to imperfection, there are punishments for that. The whole idea of patriarchy and the story of the foundation of the world have made things unequal from that time until now. There's not much anyone can do about where we find ourselves. All we can do is continue our advocacy. At least you can see some rays of light at the end of the tunnel.

What is the power of education for girls in global development?

Melinda Gates: I write in my book, *The Moment of Lift*, about a ten-year-old girl named Sona from an impoverished community in India. My colleague Gary was in her village, Kanpur, on behalf of our foundation. Sona went right up to him, handed him a little gift, and told him, 'I want a teacher.' She followed him around all day repeating those same four words: 'I want a teacher.' He looked into it, found out why she wasn't in school, and eventually some of our foundation's partners helped her get back in. When I heard that story, I was so moved by the courage Sona showed by walking up to a stranger and asking for help with her education.

Education is power and girls' education is one of the most powerful forces on the planet. If all girls received twelve years of high-quality education, women's lifetime earnings would increase by as much as $30 trillion, which is bigger than the entire US economy. We also know that the more education a woman has, the healthier her kids are. The UN estimates that if all women in low- and middle-income countries finished secondary school, child mortality in those countries would fall by about half. We know progress is possible because we've seen it. After a major push to close the gender gap in education, most countries are now enrolling nearly equal numbers of boys and girls in primary school. But there are still gender gaps when it comes to secondary education, especially in sub-Saharan Africa and parts of Asia.

What would be your message to the generation of women and girls following ours?

Leymah Gbowee: Never despise humble beginnings. You can start by sitting on your front porch with a girl. In ten years, you may see that she's gone on to do great things and she will look back on her life and say, 'It was those five minutes a day I sat on this woman's porch and interacted with her.' No matter where you come from or where you started, know that your humble beginning will lead you to great things.

Laura Bates: You are not alone, there are thousands of us behind you. We're in this exciting and positive moment with such potential for change. More young women than ever before are coming forward, helping each other and standing up for one another and carrying out incredible campaigns for change. You're not alone, you're on the right side of history, and when people get angry and try to silence you it's because they're afraid of your power and your potential. This is hard, it's a battle, but it's a battle we will win, and young women who get involved now will look back and be incredibly proud of what they achieved.

Are you hopeful? And how do you remain hopeful?

Melinda Gates: Very much so. I used to call myself an optimist, but my late friend Hans Rosling suggested that maybe a more accurate term is possibilist. His definition of a possibilist is 'someone who neither hopes without reason, nor fears without reason; someone who constantly resists the overdramatic world view'. I guess you could say that a possibilist is an evidence-based optimist. I've spent the last twenty years or so travelling to some of the world's poorest places to deepen my understanding of what life is like there. It never gets any easier to confront the realities of poverty and disease – and it shouldn't. It's important to bear witness to people's lives and suffering, and it's important to let your heart break. But that same work has also brought me into contact with extraordinary people who are devoting their ideas, their resources, even their lives to fighting poverty and disease and tearing down the barriers holding women and girls back. They do this work every day because they believe progress is possible. I'm doing everything I can to stand behind them because I do, too.

Jameela Jamil: We need to treat the impact of media and social media on women in a similar way to the public health approach to tobacco. We've got to a situation where women cannot find lives of moderation; I've seen it in my own friends who only eat too much, or too little – and feel psychologically impacted by the rhetoric. Shaming culture is unhealthy, it's unproductive and it's costing lives and life-years. It feels like this is the patriarchy's way of making us take our eyes off the ball. Think about it: it's a genius way to distract and rob us, simultaneously. If we're spending every minute of the day worrying about our looks, we're not thinking about business, studying or mental health. We're not progressing. Is this because the patriarchy feel that if we become too confident and comfortable, if we stop waking up an hour earlier than men to get ready, if we stop eating less and sleeping more, that maybe we'll have more fuel, more power, more confidence and challenge them? Look at how they treated Hillary Clinton and said she didn't smile enough! Why do women have to smile all the time? What have we got to smile about at the moment? We're having our birth control rights taken away, millions of us are being treated as second-rate citizens, we're in gender despair. Why the fuck should we smile all the time? We are just supposed to be pleasing on the eye of straight males. That is the story we're told from as soon as we can understand. It's smiley Barbie. We just have to be smiley Barbie for ever.

As I write this, there are seventy-two countries and jurisdictions where same-sex relations are criminal acts, punishable with penalties ranging from a few years in prison to life imprisonment and even the death penalty. Just think about that for a moment and realize how utterly arbitrary it is to legislate against who you can love, marry and have sex with. The way LGBT+ communities have been treated is one of the greatest inconsistencies and inequities in a world that claims to have a human rights agenda. To understand more about one of the most pressing issues of our modern times, I spoke to two of the most prominent campaigners in the field.

What is the relationship between sexuality and identity?

Ruth Hunt: The notion of identity, of who we are, has become profoundly more important in the last decade. It's become more important for people to be able to be unequivocal about who they are through a range of different labels – labels which are often then signalled through social media and other means.

What we've done, however, is include protected characteristics as part of that narrative and begun to narrow the focus of 'I' as an identity, creating a rigidity that doesn't really give people the space to change. When we look at sexuality and gender identity, we've moved away from sexuality relating to something that you *do* to something that you *are*. My identity as a lesbian is no longer just defined by my relationship to a member of the same sex, but comes with other identity factors – cultural, societal, social. And that's a real positive because the root of prejudice is often overly preoccupied with what LGBT people do rather than who they are.

What is the link between LGBT+ persecution and human rights?

Peter Tatchell: The principles of human rights are universal and indivisible. They apply to every person on the planet. If you read Articles 1 and 2 of the United Nations Universal Declaration of Human Rights, it's very clear that the right to equal treatment and non-discrimination applies to everyone – no ifs, no buts, no exceptions and no excuses. Historically, even many human rights defenders never saw LGBT+ rights as part of the human rights spectrum. But the emerging consensus is that, based on the principle of universal human rights, LGBT+ individuals should receive the same human rights protections as everyone else. The struggle to get to that point has been long and hard. Even in the United Nations, at the Human Rights Council, for many years there was a point-blank majority refusal to entertain LGBT+ rights as human rights. It's only since Kofi Annan was Secretary General that the UN had a leader who spoke out for LGBT+ rights in a consistent and sustained way. It was as recently as 2008 that the UN General Assembly first considered LGBT+ rights and even then only 67 out of 193 countries endorsed a statement condemning discrimination and violence against LGBT+ communities.

Are you hopeful for the future?

Peter Tatchell: History moves like snakes and ladders. It moves forward two steps and then back one – but despite the setback it is still one step forward. Sometimes, as we saw during Nazism, we can take *many* steps back, but the overall trajectory of human history has been towards greater human rights. Despite the faults with our world, people are on average better off economically and socially. Things aren't as equal as they should be, but compared to fifty years ago, we've certainly made great strides to expand and extend equality.

When it comes to LGBT+ rights, the big flaw in the equal rights agenda is that it implies that we merely want to assimilate and integrate within the dominant heterosexual society. It implies we LGBTs have nothing to offer or contribute to society. It suggests that we simply want to fit in with mainstream straight culture as it exists; that we accept the dominant social norms and do not dissent from them. Some people may want that. But there are many things about LGBT+ culture that straight people could learn from. The average gay and bisexual man does not mirror traditional hetero masculinity. We've evolved a new way of being a man. I'm not saying that we're not masculine, but that most gay men don't have the same machismo and toxic masculinity that has been historically associated with male heterosexuality. We're more in touch with our feelings and perhaps that's why there are a disproportionate number of gay and bisexual men who work in the creative and caring professions. Conversely, lesbian women have made a disproportionate contribution to women's advancement, being very prominent in the suffragette movement a century ago and in the 1970s battle for women to access training and work in manual trades. By breaking into those male-only occupations, they opened up new opportunities for all women, regardless of their sexuality or gender identity. In these senses, LGBT+ people have made a positive contribution to society and we've developed insights that straight people could learn from.

In this century, abuse and discrimination are rife on the internet. Social media in particular has given a platform to hate speech. During the 2016 referendum on the United Kingdom's membership of the EU as just one example, I received a cacophony of abuse and racism online from the vocal minority who felt the debate around immigration was, in fact, an open licence for them to abuse people of colour. Comedian and author David Baddiel, and the author Matt Haig, both spoke to me very eloquently about online abuse and the negative impact of social media.

How has human nature followed us online?

David Baddiel: It's interesting and frightening that we see the same behaviours online and offline. Our online life (for better or worse) constitutes a huge amount of our real life these days and the way that discourse exists online blends into real life. A concrete example is the election of Donald Trump. A man like

Trump would never have been president without social media, and that's not just because he's on Twitter a lot. The voice of Donald Trump – arrogant, stupid, without empathy – is the voice of a troll, and that adds a very large constituency when it comes from social media. People with that kind of voice have found an identity on social media – not just on Twitter, but on Reddit, 4Chan and the many other places where trolls exist. Some people like to say that none of this matters, that it's just ranting on a website, nothing to do with the real world. There's an old-hat idea that 'it just happens in the bubble of social media'. It's not as simple as that. People get far too upset about stuff that perhaps doesn't have a life outside Twitter, but I think the bleeding of the anger and the polarization that you see on Twitter into real life is an absolute real thing.

What can we do to curb social media abuse?

David Baddiel: The platforms have a very ambiguous attitude towards hate and lies online. They come from the position that everything that can be put on the internet should be put on the internet. If someone had come to you or me twenty years ago and said, 'There's going to be this technology that is going to allow everybody to share everything and see into each other's lives,' we would have said, 'Oh wow! That's amazing!' We would have assumed it would increase the sum total of truth in the world. But it's done the opposite. It's increased the sum of lies, because people don't tell the truth – they tell their truth, curated truths, and the sum of propaganda-esque truth.

Platforms don't like taking people or content off, partly because they have a financial model based on having as many people and as much content as possible – but also because they simply do not have the technology to do it. There is a quote used by anti-Semites, mistakenly attributed to Voltaire, which goes, 'To know who rules over you, simply find out who you are not allowed to criticize.' It has been shown on Twitter before with the image of a hand, with a Star of David, crushing people. It's become a code for the anti-Semites online, and now they often use the quote without an image and it's obviously very difficult for an algorithm to spot that. It's also important to realize that it's not just about trolls who are angry and give abuse, it's about mob mentality, about moralistic pile-ons. People who go on Twitter and say, 'Oh fuck off, I hate you,' are much less important than those who think they are on the side of right and truth. Everything terrible in this world has been done by people who think they are on the side of angels.

How do our news and social media cycles impact on mental health?

Matt Haig: Fear is a very, very strong emotion. We experienced fear for real reasons of our own survival as we evolved as a species, but I think fear is used in cynical ways. It's obviously used in cynical ways by terrorists – the whole idea behind creating terror is to make you feel fear. But it's also used in all kinds of other ways. We are surrounded by things that are trying to make us anxious.

Marketers use the acronym 'FUD' which stands for Fear, Uncertainty and Doubt. Marketers try to make us feel doubt, they try to make us feel fearful, whether it's anti-ageing products to make us worry about growing old, whether it's insurance, whether it's politicians trying to make us feel anxious. Fear is a very strong emotion, and it's very easy to manipulate. Our news cycle plays on this too. When something terrifying happens, we experience it in a different way to how we did before; we experience it in real time. We almost experience it as if we were there in a way we never did when we would only consume news twice a day. It just turns inwards and it even leads to destructive political behaviour or mental illness.

☼☼

With the charity In Place of War, I visit changemakers around the world who are facing oppression, marginalization and discrimination. In practically all cases we see that activism and protest are two of the most powerful tools to create change. Without a doubt, social media has amplified much of the toxicity in society, but technology also enables movements in a profoundly powerful way, not just allowing groups to organize and communicate, but allowing the world to see their message. In the year 2000, it would have been unthinkable that protesters would have been able to overthrow or challenge the authoritarian leaders of the Arab world, for example, but in the 2010s, with the start of the Arab Spring, that is exactly what happened.

☼☼

Why do we need activism in society?

L. A. Kauffman: Citizen activism has always acted as a corrective on governments, particularly those governments which only represent a small minority rather than a broad majority. History shows us time and time again that when established institutions become unresponsive or undermine people's rights, activism has been the way that people have been able to make gains or protect those they already have.

What has been the role of art in political and social conversation?

Ai Weiwei: Today, art has a wider definition. Art can be made up of its elements: form, light, colour, or a line. But it can also be a design, an expression of an attitude, or a conceptual statement. If we understand this, then art is deeply rooted in our human activity. Artists themselves may not be conscious of the broad existence of art. Museums and art academies are often stuck in the past, chewing the leftovers of aesthetic judgements passed on from their grandparents. This old habit has been difficult to quit and we still see this antiquated understanding reflected in galleries and on museum walls.

Where do you find the courage to fight?

Gad Saad: My personhood does not allow me to be exposed to bullshit, to endure attacks on truth and to not respond. I am personally offended by falsehoods in the true sense of the word 'offence', not as a manifestation of the culture of victimhood. I am psychically injured when I see the endless attacks on truth and that carries more weight in my personal conduct than careerist aspirations. Am I just being a martyr? No. When I go to bed at night and I lay my head down, before I fall asleep I need to feel that there is nothing that I could have done that I chose not to do because I was cowardly. That allows me to go to sleep because I've cleared my very high threshold of what I consider to be proper personal conduct. You have to set your bar high enough to be defending the truth rather than your own selfish goals. Look, all the people in the world that have affected profound change looked beyond themselves, right?

Great people rise to the occasion. You don't have to be great in that you become a famous professor, but you could be great in your personal conduct, so when you lay your head down on your pillow you can say 'I did all that I could'. Until we can foster that exacting personal conduct in everyone, they will keep deflecting the responsibility onto the few of us and then we will lose the battle of ideas.

What would be your advice to the next generation of activists?

Ai Weiwei: I have no advice because my experiences are limited to my time. That time will change and the next generation will face very different tests. However, they should understand that without meaningful struggle, the word 'freedom' is empty and life would be lived in vain.

L. A. Kauffman: Protest works when it's done with intelligence. You have to be willing to use the stronger tools of citizen engagement if you want to make an impact, particularly when the odds seem against you. Within the toolbox of non-violent direct action, there are a huge number of tools you can use, including rallies, speak-outs, blockades, sit-ins, and other more disruptive ones. At a moment when the threats are so severe and unrelenting, we need to look at that toolbox as a whole, and use all the methods we can, collectively, to get the change we need.

⚙☼

The word 'discrimination' is interesting. In the most literal sense, it refers to the act of making distinctions, of observing, or marking a difference. This may seem innocent enough, but the reality is that discrimination has become one of the greatest weapons in modern society.

Race has been one of the most common dividing lines used to separate us, and as Dexter Dias QC told me, it's a concept that simply does not exist in science or biology. Research shows that we are all, in fact, just African migrants with a different trajectory. I may 'identify' as Indian, but from sequencing my own DNA, I know that my ancestry traces back to Haplogroup L (maternal line) and Haplogroup A (paternal line). I am the long-lost child of two East Africans who lived almost 200,000 years ago – as are you, as all of us are. That is the beautiful truth of our existence, yet the myth of race was meticulously assembled to divide us, to organize us, and sometimes to exploit us. By creating race, we denied our shared humanity, and all of us are poorer as a result. Race is not the only dividing line, however. Whether it's gender, sexuality, ability, income, political leaning, religion, caste, class or any of the other arbitrary tags we attach to ourselves – we find ourselves divided, and conquered.

It took the immediate horrors of two world wars (not to mention the conflicts before) for the world to adopt a universal declaration of human rights and, as Peter Tatchell said, those rights are universal and indivisible, they apply to every person on the planet. Front and centre of that declaration, Article 1 and Article 2 are the principles that not only are all human beings born free and equal in dignity and rights, but that they are all entitled to the rights and freedoms associated with equal treatment, without discrimination. This is a non-negotiable – no ifs, no exceptions and no excuses. Yet we continue to see discrimination and marginalization of our fellow human beings, causing suffering, loss of life and economic hardship because, while we have enshrined these rights to paper, we have yet to grow up as a society and live them.

Ending discrimination is not a social or cultural issue; it's a matter of justice. We are no longer in the protracted infancy of our pre-industrialized lives. We are a technologically, socially and culturally complex species with the power and weaponry to extinguish ourselves. With that in mind, it makes sense that the best thing for all of us is to cooperate and make peace with each other. Although, as the German sociologist and philosopher Theodor Adorno identified, 'Human progress can be summed up as the advance from the spear to the guided missile, showing that though we have grown cleverer, we have certainly not grown wiser.' For there to be true equality, the concept of 'justice' must be interpreted and applied holistically – society is, after all, based on the principle that social cooperation makes possible a better life for all than any would have if each were to live solely by their own efforts.

Industrialization may be considered our adolescence, but society has surely now come of age and has strength through the creativity, innovation, technological and intellectual endeavour, which has provided us (predominantly in the occidental nations) with economic opportunity and greater wealth than at any point in human history. This has made society 'clever', but the gaping injustices we see now place us at a unique precipice in our story, where we need to understand that we are in this together. Society, as writer and philosopher Ayn Rand identified, is the 'process of setting man free from men'. A view echoed by Rose McGowan, who described how we need to unlearn what we've learned, and view the world through the eyes of the other and not simply adhere to the cult and echo chambers of ignorance. And as Walter Cronkite observes, and allows me to conclude, 'there is no such thing as a little freedom. Either you are all free, or you are not free.'

BIOGRAPHIES

David Baddiel is a British American comedian, author, screenwriter and television presenter.

Laura Bates is a feminist writer and author, and founded the Everyday Sexism Project website in 2012, a collection of more than 80,000 women's daily experiences of gender inequality.

Lord John Bird MBE is a social entrepreneur and life peer. He is the co-founder of *The Big Issue* and is also the founder of the International Network of Street Papers.

Sir Philip Craven MBE is a former Paralympic wheelchair basketball player, and was president of the International Paralympic Committee (IPC) from 2001 to 2017.

Frederik Willem (F. W.) de Klerk is a South African politician and former State President of South Africa. He and his government dismantled the apartheid system and introduced universal suffrage, for which he was awarded a joint Nobel Peace Prize with Nelson Mandela.

Dexter Dias QC is an author and award-winning international human rights lawyer. He has acted in some of the most high-profile cases in recent years involving freedom of expression, murder, crimes against humanity, terrorism, FGM and genocide.

Melinda Gates is an American philanthropist. She is the former general manager at Microsoft and co-founder of the Bill and Melinda Gates Foundation, one of the world's largest private charitable organizations.

Leymah Gbowee is a Liberian peace activist. She was the leader of Women of Liberia Mass Action for Peace, a non-violent peace movement that helped bring an end to the Second Liberian Civil War in 2003. In 2011 she was awarded a Nobel Peace Prize for her work.

Matt Haig is a British author. His bestselling memoir, *Reasons to Stay Alive*, stayed in the British top ten for forty-six weeks. He has received many awards and has been nominated for the Carnegie Medal three times.

Afua Hirsch is a writer, author, presenter, documentary maker and former barrister. She is currently the Wallis Annenberg Chair of Journalism at the University of Southern California in Los Angeles.

Baroness Ruth Hunt is former Chief Executive of Stonewall, the UK's largest charity campaigning to improve equality for lesbian, gay, bisexual and transgender people. She is a cross-bench peer in the House of Lords and co-director of Deeds and Words.

Jameela Jamil is a British actress, presenter, model, writer and activist. She most recently starred in Mike Schur's series for NBC, *The Good Place*, opposite Ted Danson and Kristen Bell.

L. A. Kauffman is an American activist and journalist.

Her writing focuses on the history and impact of protest movements, including the civil rights movement and the 2017 Women's March.

Iby Knill BEM is an author and Holocaust survivor. She has written a book on her experiences, *The Woman Without a Number.*

Rose McGowan is an American actress, activist and *New York Times* bestselling author. She was named one of *Time* magazine's people of the year in 2017.

Dr Gad Saad is a professor, evolutionary behavioural scientist, author and host of the YouTube show *The SAAD Truth.*

Harry Leslie Smith (1923–2018) was an English writer and political commentator, and served in the Royal Air Force during the Second World War.

George Takei is an American actor, author and activist. He is best known for his role in the television series *Star Trek* and for his activism and advocacy for human rights.

Peter Tatchell is a British human rights campaigner. He has been campaigning for LGBT+ and other human rights for over fifty years. He is the current director of the Peter Tatchell Foundation.

Ai Weiwei is a Chinese contemporary artist and activist. He has received many honours for his art and activism, including Amnesty International's Ambassador of Conscience Award in 2015.

ON CONFLICT: WAR, PEACE AND JUSTICE

'The mechanisms of conflict resolution or conciliation often don't come into play until wars are in play, or until they have got to impossible positions, and that is, I think, the sad thing about so many conflicts.'

BERTIE AHERN

It's 2019, and I'm in the north of Uganda with a team from our international charity, In Place of War. It's perhaps fitting that the soil was red with ferrous metals, a reminder that the ground under our feet had witnessed decades of brutal mechanized conflicts, from the coup launched by Idi Amin Dada in 1971, the civil war against Obote's government in 1981 and the twenty-year-long fight between Uganda and the Lord's Resistance Army, led by Kony and his top commanders. This latter conflict ravaged northern Uganda, southern Sudan and eastern Congo, making the region for a while one of the most dangerous places on earth. Tens of thousands have been left permanently traumatized and physically disabled, and 1.5 million people were driven from their pastoral existences into the squalor of refugee camps, where they lived for almost twenty years. This was a war the international community barely paid attention to because of the neighbouring crises in Darfur, Rwanda, Congo, Somalia and western Sudan – and one that has disrupted indigenous communities across the nation. Uganda has been at peace for a relatively short time, and when our charity first arrived over a decade ago, we were facing a reality where rural communities, devastated by war, were still finding landmines while they were planting the crops they needed to survive.

Speaking to the communities in Gulu and Kitgum, I encountered generations for whom war was a fact of life. Today, Uganda is at peace, but it's a fragile peace held together by the collective sense that the nation has heard enough gunfire, and now wants to move forward and create a new narrative. This is the same reality we see in Colombia, Venezuela, Palestine, the Democratic Republic of Congo, Kenya, Sudan, Syria, South Africa, Brazil and so many other places where the exhaustion of conflict is replaced by a collective need to rebuild and move on, together with a wish for some sense of justice. Estimates state that in the 3,500 years of recorded history, there have only been 270 years of peace. One could argue, therefore, that conflict is an essential part of human nature, and that its absence is an anomaly. But what is the reality of conflict and war in our society, and what are the chances that we will ever see a world at peace?

In this chapter are some of the conversations I've had with individuals who have shaped society's return from conflict and, in some cases, been through it themselves. Dr Shirin Ebadi, former presidents Martti Ahtisaari and Lech Wałęsa, and Professor Jody Williams all received the Nobel Peace Prize for their work, ranging from negotiating peace deals to ending the use of weapons of mass destruction, and Zeid Ra'ad Al Hussein acted as UN High Commissioner for Human Rights alongside being President of the UN Security Council. I also spoke to Ben Ferencz, one of the last living prosecutors from the Nuremberg trials, and Gulwali Passarlay who, as a refugee from conflict, has experienced modern warfare and the impact it has on communities.

Why do war and conflict exist in society?

Shirin Ebadi: War remains humanity's most profitable trait and we see that many economic crises have been resolved through war. Many people lose their lives simply to enable the rich to become richer.

Martti Ahtisaari: Thinking on this question I start to wonder as to why we have not seen any such conflicts in my country (Finland). We have been at peace for over seventy years. We have been living in relative unanimity for many years. People feel that institutions work for them and that civil servants work for them. There is trust between people and institutions, and many enjoy more than 80 per cent support. In different parts of the world we see a raw and uncontrollable desire for power, where people create wars and conflicts. If you have enormous inequality, it easily creates conditions where violence is the only way out. We have enough statistical evidence to show that fair and just societies have less violence.

Lech Wałęsa: Conflicts exist where there are poorly developed regions. Where there is still a problem with basic needs. These developmental differences cause conflicts. In the old days, humanity struggled for the land, to make their country bigger, and so I call this epoch the Era of

Land. Now in modern civilization, where we spend more money for intellectual things than for food and clothes, we become merchants to other nations. They are not interested in eliminating us. They need us to buy their goods, cars, computers etc. If we equal the development levels, the risk of conflicts will be much lower.

Bertie Ahern: Armed conflict is an anathema to how the world should work, but often it's the result of unsurmountable issues that cannot be resolved by negotiations, or because people don't put the effort into conciliation, arbitration or dialogue. We frequently see conflicts that occur as a result of governments or people that are afraid to move positions that are held due to historical differences, or bad policies. Some of our world's most protracted and brutal armed conflicts are also the result of governments, in nations with vast mineral resources, giving contracts out to other countries or private companies, without consulting or involving people on the ground, or locally – the Niger Delta is a typical example of just such a conflict. Unfortunately, the mechanisms of conflict resolution or conciliation often don't come into play until wars are in play, or until they have got to impossible positions, and that is, I think, the sad thing about so many conflicts.

What causes peace to break down?

Zeid Ra'ad Al Hussein: There is hardly an armed conflict today which doesn't have its roots in the gross violation of human rights. How many conflicts can you think of which are a straightforward boundary dispute and nothing else, that have no relation to repressive measures or the rights agenda? There's not one I can think of. All of them have their roots in the denial of basically rights, fundamental freedoms and the deprivation of those that rides on the back of their denial. Economists have a way of looking at these issues using a euphemistic lexicon. They talk of exclusion and inclusion in a way that's so antiseptic that you don't question it. The reality is that exclusion is often made up of deliberate racism, chauvinistic policies, bigotry and other ingredients that cannot be represented in a pseudo-benign fashion. When we talk of inclusive policies and inclusive economics, we need to confront whoever is excluding parts of society from the labour market and say, 'You cannot do this.'

People have this misguided notion that exclusion is because changes in technology and investment patterns have caused people to fall off the employment cart, and that we must therefore get them back on. In many countries, these people were never on the employment cart. They were always excluded. Then there are the migrants, those fleeing conflict and climate change, the people affected by austerity. You see the same when you examine those who bear the brunt of disease burden in society – it's always the same. Human rights are not taken as seriously as they should be. The interests of the elites dominate economies, and the structure, and security, of our countries are being protected for those elites at the cost of the interests of the rest.

Are conflict and violence a part of human nature?

Shirin Ebadi: Just as aggression and envy can be inherent in all human beings, the same can be said of violence and war. It is possible through education and training to harness these inherent sensations in human beings and prevent them. Unfortunately, in the schools of today, lessons of history tend to praise war rather than condemn it. Personally, I think it's very important to change school curriculums if we want to change the status quo.

Martti Ahtisaari: If it was not a part of human nature, we would not have these conflicts in the first place. There are also, however, practical reasons for conflict. It may be that some people have lost their land or water through climate change or land-grabbing. I don't think it makes it any more justifiable to draw arms in these situations, but it can explain why these occasions occur.

Ahtisaari's view, that war is part of human nature, may seem controversial as we all believe we are 'good' people, but it's easy to forget how complex and fragile the bonds that hold society together really are. We, like all other animals, are naturally prone to conflict and it takes the bonds we build as a society, and the culture we lay on top of that, to push back against those primal instincts. For society to remain peaceful, we cannot be blind to these basic human natures, nor so fragile that we cannot acknowledge that violent conflict can rarely be justified.

Can war or conflict ever be justified?

Jody Williams: I debate this a lot. As we sit here, a big point of contention is a potential military response to Syria's supposed use of chemical weapons in the civil war. Can that be justified? Or has the US backed itself into a corner by stating that there is a red line that cannot be crossed and now that it has been crossed, are they left without a choice? If we look at the US and its military actions in the Middle East and North Africa – bombing Libya, drone strikes in Yemen and Somalia, invasion of Iraq, involvement in the Iran–Iraq war, and so on – it's hard to imagine how anyone from that region or with ties to that region could think of the US as anything other than an outright aggressor with no moral high ground. I suppose the biggest example of a justified war, and one that is always waved out there, is the Second World War, but have any wars been justified since that time? I'm not so sure.

Shirin Ebadi: Hitherto in my life, I have not come across an eventuality in which war can be justified, because war breeds violence. If you look at the history of the past twenty years, wherever there has been a war, it has never been followed by peace and tranquillity. For instance, look at Iraq, Libya and Afghanistan.

Martti Ahtisaari: War can be justified when it is a defensive one. I am an eternally displaced person, luckily in my own country. I was two years of age when the Soviet Union attacked Finland, and we lost 11 per cent of our land, but we were never occupied. Four hundred thousand of us from Karjalohja where I come from, including my family and relatives, had to be resettled in the rest of Finland. That, I regard as our right. Many countries in our neighbourhood decided to do otherwise, but I'm very proud that we defended ourselves. In 1918, the first year of our independence, Finland had a civil war. We fought against each other. This may have been a reflection of our conflict with Russia, but there were also many complaints. Farmers did not have land and inequality was very high. We got out of that and became an inclusive society where everyone had a chance to participate in the political process. In ten years, those who lost the war were eventually in government. It was the Social Democrats who were pushing for egalitarian policies, but a long time ago every political party accepted. The whole of society felt it was good to give every child a fair opportunity, to give them good healthcare before and after they're born, to give them a decent education wherever they live. Children do not ask to be born into poor families, so it should not matter whether they are or not – they have every right to those things.

Lech Wałęsa: Violence is always a bad choice. I always look for a peaceful method. But I understand that there can be situations in the world where, to stay alive, you need to kill someone else. We are responsible for that because we should help those who find themselves in those situations by creating a safe environment where they don't have to make that choice.

How fragile is our global order?

Zeid Ra'ad Al Hussein: It's amazing to think that it took upwards of 100 to 200 million deaths, the casualties of the First World War, Second World War and Spanish Influenza outbreak, to force us to think more like rational human beings, rather than self-interested nativists who only pursue the narrow at the expense of the broad. Progress is slow. Why is it that things that seem to be self-evident (equality, non-discrimination, anti-racism) take time to become the norm, and vast swathes of society still cling on to primitive ways of thinking? Why are we so incapable of learning the deeper lessons of our history? Cecil Lewis, an author I much admire, published a book in 1936, reflecting on his experiences of the First World War. In that book he refers to the invincibility of man's stupidity. It's very appropriate he doesn't mention women – it's men who are fundamentally stupid in this. Indeed, peace is very fragile.

What are the key causes of conflict and war?

Jody Williams: Different conflicts result from different elements of economics, politics and other social factors, or combinations thereof. Race and religion are used as tools to inflame a populace to support or engage in war. I don't think that religion in and of itself causes war. War is pretty much always about money and power. The tools that are used to get the masses to engage in war can be race, religion, or anything that can make an enemy seem as 'the other' and 'less' than 'we' are; and therefore worthy of being killed in a war. Climate change, on the other hand, does affect population flows and does contribute to conflict. If we look at the situation in Sudan and Darfur, part of this situation is down to the ongoing desertification of the region, pushing nomadic groups further and further away from where they have been historically able to raise animals and into otherwise settled populations. Economics are also very important. Many of the massive demonstrations throughout Europe have been about economic stagnation and collapse. There are certainly the seeds being sown there of violent conflict.

What is the start of the peacebuilding and reconciliation process?

Martti Ahtisaari: Conflict always leaves a mark, regardless of whether it was an internal exercise or whether external forces were involved. It becomes very clear in many cases that it's very, very difficult to start the reconciliation process. There are so many examples. In my country it was winner takes it all, but inclusive policies came, and thank God we've done well. There are still, however, people who remember what happened in their families, and there is not always the same forgiveness we have seen in South Africa. There are also examples such as Bosnia and Herzegovina where they have three distinct histories: the Croats, the Serbs and the Bosniaks. Even if you forgive, it still leaves bitterness because you cannot deal with the atrocities that have been committed.

As a peace mediator, the best I can achieve in many cases is to achieve a change of behaviour in society; to make sure people know that what's happened in the past will never be repeated. To think that I could correct all the wrongdoing in a society – wrongdoings which are very often committed by both sides – is impossible. In Northern Ireland, for example, they are largely maintaining peace, but the reconciliation process has not gone through yet. If there is a conflict, one had better be prepared that it will take a long time to correct the problems it will create. The first step is to simplify the process as much as you can. If you think that you can solve all the past atrocities, it won't happen. You have to bid for the future. This doesn't satisfy everybody, and can sometimes make it even more complicated to find peace. People feel that everything should be agreed before they sign a ceasefire. I witnessed that type of discussion in Myanmar with The Elders' Gro Harlem

Brundtland and Jimmy Carter. Very often you need peace first to start a proper dialogue on all the grievances that exist in society, and you can never solve all of them.

When I got the Nobel Peace Prize, I said that we can solve every problem and conflict in the world. I don't understand why situations as we have in Cyprus and Kashmir are still allowed to happen. I remember when I was negotiating in Kosovo, one visitor asked me why I was in a hurry as there were so many unsolved conflicts! I told him that he should never advise me or anyone else to have more frozen conflicts in the world – it's a disgrace for the international community.

Bertie Ahern: Peacebuilding is a difficult task, and sometimes it's a matter of timing. Often, war and violence are inevitable, and combatants, whether illegal groups, paramilitary or government, are not prepared to have dialogue – and it takes a long time before anyone even starts to look at a strategy for peace. There is a stage where people are beaten, when they become weary of conflict or when a hand of friendship is held out by people who try to see the bigger picture. Those are the glimmers of hope that I look for at a personal level in peacebuilding. I look for broad acceptance by the parties involved in the conflict that the status quo is untenable, and that some form of agreement is better in terms of everybody's interests. If people don't believe the status quo is untenable, and if they're not prepared to move on, there's very little you can do – and usually the conflict continues, indefinitely.

How can we create resilient peace?

Zeid Ra'ad Al Hussein: If I asked you to tell me the algorithm for the construction of peace, you wouldn't be able to tell me – there isn't one. After seventy years of peacebuilding, we still don't have one and that is a central failing of peacebuilding as a craft. We have a war in Iraq, we go in and throw cement at the problem. We train officials, we put money into rebuilding physical infrastructure, administrative infrastructure, but we never think about how we're going to cope with the narratives, the historical memory, the matters of identity. Who are the people? How do they view themselves? Why do they see that a common experience may be subject to different interpretations? If that's the case in Iraq, Bosnia and so many countries, doesn't that reveal a hole that we are utterly incapable of filling?

Look around the world today. You are seeing great passion, the tearing down of statues that represent the colonial experience of racism. It's pent-up frustration that hasn't been dealt with over time. It's just amazing to see how stupid we can be as a society, how much we put our heads in the sand when we need proper and deep dialogue. Any part of our history that may send ambivalent signals where our narrative isn't settled, we have to deal with it. You don't turn a blind eye knowing it will create and keep the divisions of society in place. We're immensely short-sighted when it comes to how we deal with the peace problem.

What is the relationship of culture and religion to conflict and peacebuilding?

Shirin Ebadi: Cross-cultural understanding is a part of the series of factors contributing to human dignity that, in turn, contribute to building peace. If I live in a society that is unable to tolerate my culture or religion, that will undermine my human dignity.

Lech Wałęsa: In our peace movement, religion was something that united us. I think that music, art, religion, culture are things that unite people, help them think and feel similarly. If the people are united, they can build whatever they want.

Are some acts unforgivable?

Marina Cantacuzino: Forgiveness is highly contested territory, as I have said, and again this is entirely personal. For some people forgiveness is conditional on remorse and apology. Others say apology or remorse might never be possible for multiple reasons and therefore if you wait for it and expect it you are simply putting the power in the wrong hands. Forgiveness, therefore, is an act of self-healing and empowerment. So, what is unforgivable for one person, may not be for the next.

Take Eva Kor, for example. It's hard to imagine how she could ever forgive the Nazi doctors, particularly Dr Josef Mengele, who experimented on her in Auschwitz as a child. And yet she does and she is very clear about what forgiveness is for her. She says, 'I forgive not because they deserve it, but because I deserve it. Forgiveness is really nothing more than an act of self-healing and self-empowerment. I call it a miracle medicine. It is free, it works and has no side effects.' Actually, the French philosopher Jacques Derrida believed that the only wrongdoing that calls for forgiveness is that which is unforgivable. By this he meant wrongs that can never be understood, overlooked or undone and therefore cannot be fixed by restitution or reconciliation.

Can forgiveness take the place of revenge?

Marina Cantacuzino: Jude Whyte, whose mother was killed in Northern Ireland by an IRA bomb during the sectarian conflict, says: 'You could say my revenge for the murder of my mother is my forgiveness because it has given me strength.' That statement tells you that, yes, forgiveness can be used as a powerful form of revenge. Some perpetrators want to keep you trapped to them, forever burdened by the pain, and forgiveness cuts the ties. Take another example, Scarlett Lewis, whose six-year-old son, Jesse, was one of twenty children murdered at the Sandy Hook elementary school massacre. She has been on a long journey towards forgiveness and says: 'Forgiveness felt like I was given a big pair of scissors to cut the tie and regain my personal power.' Once you are able to forgive the person or people who have hurt you, they no longer have control over your state of mind. As the great Irish writer Oscar Wilde said rather flippantly but very accurately, 'Forgive your enemies because nothing annoys them more.'

Lech Wałęsa: Forgiveness is a beautiful action, but to do so is not so easy. Sometimes people experience too much violence, lose families, houses and their health. It is really hard for them to forgive. The role of forgiveness is very important even if forgiveness means only to stop retaliation.

Forgiveness is hard and any of us that have ever had to forgive will know this first-hand. Even in our rather mundane lives, the act of forgiveness for relatively inconsequential wrongs can take months, sometimes years, of introspection. When we visited South Africa with our In Place of War team, we met a man who used to be a senior member of an extremely violent gang, and who had killed family members in the community he now supports. In an almost unbelievable act of generosity, the community have forgiven him, as they know that he is the best hope, through his work, of preventing their young people following the same path. Forgiveness does not have to be selfless, it does not have to be selfish, but it has to be real and sustainable.

How can we proactively apply peacebuilding techniques to societies that are becoming divided?

Bertie Ahern: Perhaps because I was involved in politics during the 1980s, 1990s and 2000s, I am a great believer in multilateralism. I have great regard and respect for the organizations that have been built up over generations and which are multilateral – the UNDP, for example. It's extremely worrying that the groundwork of multilateralism is being damaged and undermined, particularly so over the last two years. It is more important than ever, therefore, that conflict resolution organizations work together and build systems of multilateral connection almost outside the government system. This isn't ideal – it's far better when governments are prepared to play a bigger role to help fund these issues. We have countries like Norway that do great work in this sense, but it's harder than ever now because the hand of friendship is no longer being held out by all countries in an effort to resolve issues.

Will we see a world free from conflict?

Jody Williams: If people really care, then this could definitely be achieved within the lives of our children or possibly our grandchildren. It is possible! People have to stand up and say no to being cannon fodder for a few sitting in their capitals who send them to war for more power, money, resource and more.

Martti Ahtisaari: To answer this, I look at my part of the world. With the support of the population, inclusive policies and egalitarian policies, you can create an environment which gives opportunities for everyone and hence very little conflict. If you look at the percentage of the population in prison in countries such as the United States you see what happens when you don't have egalitarian policies and you can't move from one social class to another, and if education and opportunities are poor. In many cases you see families with multiple generations of poor education and opportunity, and these individuals can easily become targets for criminal gangs, drug gangs and others. One economist recently stated, 'If you want to live the American dream, go to Sweden.' Many argue that this is due to homogeneity of the Nordic countries, but this is not true. Sweden today is a less homogeneous society than the UK. There are also many old attitudes present in the world that are preventing progress. We have to send a very clear message to today's Russia, for example, that the Cold War is over. The West is no longer attempting to threaten them militarily, NATO doesn't even have the capacity to do that. It should be the least of Russia's worries. They could use that money to improve the rule of law, and the rest of the unilateral values in their society such as education. We should be much more capable of cooperating to end the conflicts we have.

Ben Ferencz: The answer to your question is very clearly no, but I don't want you to walk away with that answer, because it is deceptive. We are moving in the direction of peace – we will never have perfection and we shouldn't expect it. The fact that confined spots here and there are rotten should not misguide us into forgetting that we can make progress, we are making progress, and we have to continue to make progress. The progress we have made so far is inadequate, and the crimes that are being committed are outrageous. There's nothing you can do instantaneously to reverse what has been glorified for centuries. We have, for centuries, glorified the killing of people with whom you cannot reach an agreement – we don't yet have the answers to prevent that.

What are your greatest worries for the next generation?

Lech Wałęsa: My greatest worry is populism; we have to fight the demagogues and so-called leaders who do whatever they want without consequence. I worry what will happen if populists gain power on a massive scale; they can destroy society. We need to find an answer, a new structure for the world that is beautiful – but to do that, we must be organized and united.

What would be your message to the generation after ours to build a peaceful world?

Martti Ahtisaari: I would urge the next generation to learn from our mistakes. What worries me sometimes is that we haven't learned very much from history. We should study why we have landed into certain situations, as it would be totally possible to avoid making the same mistakes again. It's sad to see how much the populist movements get supported in today's Europe. It's a totally unintellectual debate we see that leads people to make those choices. I have learned in my life that it's important to know the facts. You have to be able to analyse a situation and understand what is really behind it. Populism has no room for this approach. The younger generation are much brighter than mine, and I have hope for them in the future.

Lech Wałęsa: Our generation destroyed old roles, opened the borders in Europe, united Europe, and we opened a new era for your generation. New eras need new structures, new ways of thinking, and you have to rebuild everything for a new era. You have to understand that developments in technology brought us to a point where our weapons can destroy the whole world, so the only way forward for the future is to build peace and unite nations.

Ben Ferencz: After the war, we captured in Berlin records where the Nazi commanders at the front had been proudly reporting to their headquarters how many Jews, Gypsies and other opponents they had murdered. They never used the term 'murdered', but 'eliminated'. I consolidated those reports (I did it on a little adding machine) and when I realized that a million people had been killed, I flew with that evidence down from Berlin to Nuremberg with my boss, and said, 'You've got to put on a new trial.' He said, 'We can't; there's lawyers already assigned, we can't authorize new trials.' He said, 'Can you do it in addition to your other work?' And I said, 'Sure.' So he appointed me and I became the Chief Prosecutor to the largest murder trial in human history. I was twenty-seven years old. For fifty years I then tried to work in getting a permanent international court set up, and we finally did it. The International Criminal Court now exists at The Hague.

When the ICC got to their first trial, a modern case, the Chief Prosecutor called me up and said, 'Ben, we'd like you to do the closing statement for the prosecution.' And I said, 'Of course I will.' And so, aged ninety-two, I went and made the closing statement for the prosecution. I'm now in my ninety-eighth year, so that is simply to give you some feeling of the time it takes to go forward, and I'm still working on this – seven days a week, fifteen hours every day, trying to continue this work of creating a more rational humane world. We have basically got to change the hearts and minds of people, particularly the young people. Young people are the court of public opinion; they are the people who will say, 'Hell no, we won't go.' The world is much more dangerous than it has been. We have the capacity from cyberspace now to cut off the electrical grid on planet earth. We don't have to invent such ridiculous terms as 'collateral damage' as though it was just a passing wind. Today's weapons can kill everybody, or wipe out our whole city by just cutting off utilities without a sound. This is the world we're looking at. We have to have effective mechanisms to settle disputes, no matter what they are, without war. War should be treated with the contempt it deserves, and not glorified. War is hell. I was there; I've seen it, experienced it and lived it.

Our governments aren't fighting to end war – we still have diplomats who are quibbling and competing over who can build the most effective weapon to kill the most people. In my ninety-eighth year, it's not my problem. But for the younger people, wake up, speak up, stop it! To the young people of today, I give them three pieces of advice: one, never give up. Two, never give up. Three, never give up. And that's the best advice I can give, and I am hopeful as I view the progress which has been significant over the years with the creation of the courts and the awakening of the human conscience. We are making good progress, but we have a long way still to go and it's getting more dangerous every day. We mustn't be blinded by the problems and thereby ignore the progress. The progress we have seen since the Second World War is very significant. We do have courts, we are teaching international criminal law in universities all around the world, we do have various declarations of human rights which are not honoured in full but nevertheless have had an impact.

Shirin Ebadi: Those seeking peace in their society must remember that what you wish for yourself, you should wish for others, and that what harms you also harms others. That would be my message for the next generation, or for any individuals who wish to create peace in their society.

There is nothing new about human displacement from war. The very word refugee can be traced back to the French *réfugié*, a description given to the Protestants who fled France following the revocation of the Edict of Nantes (1685) – a law that granted religious liberty and civil rights to the Protestants (Huguenots) for over a century. In the years that followed, it is estimated that close to 500,000 French Protestants left France. The cultural confusion of those who migrate because they want to, for say, a new job, versus those who are displaced due to conflict or famine, has created yet another form of discriminatory language and labelling, another easy group for us to otherize and blame for our social ills. It is not necessarily that we have a refugee crisis, but rather a crisis in our understanding of those who flee for their lives.

What is the scale of our global migration and refugee movement?

Alexander Betts: Today, we have around 260 million international migrants in the world, up from about 70 million in 1970. Interestingly, the proportion of the world's total population that is migrating has been relatively constant, at around 3 per cent since the 1970s. So, the proportion of the world's population migrating has not changed dramatically. What has been increasing, though, is the number of people displaced by conflict or persecution. We have around 60 million people displaced around the world today, more than at any time since the Second World War, and more than 22 million of these people are refugees who have fled across a border. The difficulty is that the legal definition of a refugee (created in the aftermath of the Second World War) was a person fleeing persecution. This was an era in which most people were fleeing from East to West during the early Cold War – they were individuals being targeted by the state. Today, though, the primary reason for people fleeing is that they have come from fragile states, some of which are in conflict and have wars. Others are just chronically weak states that can't provide for the basic needs of their people; societies like Somalia, Iraq, Afghanistan, Central African Republic, and the Democratic Republic of Congo. This is where you get into the grey area of people fleeing for reasons of survival but without necessarily fitting neatly into the legal definition of a refugee.

Catherine Woollard: From 2014 to 2015, we saw a quadrupling of the number of people arriving into Europe, with around 1 million people arriving in 2015. That provoked an extraordinary political crisis in Europe, even though those numbers were very manageable for the continent. Only 17 per cent of those forcibly displaced are in Europe, and that includes Turkey – which is the world's largest refugee-hosting country. Thirty per cent of those forcibly displaced are in Africa and we see major refugee-hosting countries like Uganda, Kenya and Ethiopia, places far poorer than the European continent. We've seen a disproportionate focus on Europe and a reaction that doesn't really represent the real situation of displacement.

George Rupp: There are over 65 million uprooted people in the world today. Around two-thirds of them are internally displaced, which means that they are still within their own countries of origin. Some 20 million have crossed international borders and therefore are technically, in UN terminology, refugees. But all of them have experienced similar problems, have been uprooted from their homes, and are having to figure out how to support themselves and their families and find security.

I'm ever conscious of the consequences of labelling a group, so I asked Professor Rupp whether it was fair to refer to the current state and volumes of refugee movements as a problem.

I think it's perfectly fine to call it a problem. It is a problem. It is also a movement, but not one that is altogether voluntary. The scale in statistical terms is that there are over 65 million uprooted people in the world today.

What are the obligations of countries towards refugees?

Catherine Woollard: The Refugee Convention of 1951 and its 1967 protocol state the obligations on asylum, and protection of people who have fled due to persecution. Within Europe, obligations are codified in European asylum law – the Common European Asylum System – which sets the standards that member states (and associated non-member states) must adhere to in terms of standards of reception, what people are entitled to and what happens when they arrive, the right to make asylum claims and so on. It also includes the right to a fair asylum procedure. There are also rights to family reunion.

How can we improve the situation for our refugees?

Gulwali Passarlay: Helping refugees isn't rocket science; you just need compassion in the political world. You have 65 million refugees and displaced people in our world, roughly the same as the UK population. What people need to understand is that the majority of these people are either in the same country, or near the region they left. The majority of countries taking refugees are not in the Western world – they are places like Jordan, Pakistan, Turkey and Kenya. One in ten people at most from this group end up in Europe. But guess what – we only call it a crisis when it gets to Europe. We only call it a crisis when trucks are delayed or holidays are delayed. The global community has not taken its responsibilities towards refugees seriously; we're not helping countries host refugees and provide education and healthcare. Countries pledge to give money, and that money never materializes.

Citizens are, in general, very compassionate. I travel across Britain doing talks at schools, at universities. People are very compassionate, people want to show solidarity, to foster, to welcome strangers into their home. It's just the government who are lacking. At the moment we have a hostile environment where everyone who comes to our country is seen like a suspect, as a liar, as a criminal. With refugees, they are guilty until proven innocent. It is not the other way around. We're not innocent until proven guilty. The system is very dehumanizing it's inhumane, it's immoral, it treats you not as a human, it makes you feel subhuman. We need to take our fair share; we're not doing enough. And the refugee crisis is not going to go away. We ought to take responsibility, and I think it's our moral duty. It's our legal obligation to do something about this crisis.

François Crépeau: Change will take time, maybe the passing of at least a generation, but we must work with those who carry today the voice of migrants. In recent times, film directors and novelists have been telling us about mobility and diversity. The whole stream of science fiction is about this. *Star Trek* is all about mobility and diversity, going where no man has gone before, encountering new species and understanding them. Novels like *Brick Lane* by Monica Ali, or, more recently, documentary films like *Human Flows* by Ai Weiwei, show the way forward. Artists are much more forward-looking in the migration debate than politicians: they already sense and predict what the challenges of tomorrow are going to be, just like *Guernica* by Picasso forecasted the Second World War.

Lawyers, human rights institutions and churches have been working with migrants for decades and have pushed their voice into the courts, but very few migrants go to court, protest, contest or demonstrate in the streets. They fear being detected, detained and deported. Migrants have suffered too much to risk their whole migration project crumble by sticking their neck out. Their preferred strategy is to duck any blow that endangers the migration project and move on to another place or another job.

Protesting, contesting, demonstrating means risking being detected as undocumented or a troublemaker, as well as taking time and energy out of the immediate goal of sending back money to the family or creating a future for oneself and one's children. Migrant workers with a precarious status are at the very bottom of the pit in terms of social capital: they have little social connections, they have no family network, they do not speak the language. They are in the same ecological niche as the industrial workers of the nineteenth century, the indentured labour of the colonial era, or slaves of former eras. Unions have often historically been hostile to migrants, seeing them as competition for their members. Some unions now understand that migrant labour is an untapped pool of future members, for example in the agricultural sector. But unions are facing a deregulated labour market and a de-unionizing political atmosphere, where collective bargaining is seen as a swear word.

Do we need a world without borders?

Alexander Betts: Today, the rich privileged elite live in a world which is effectively borderless, yet people from poorer societies have huge restrictions and boundaries on their travel. Inequality is a defining characteristic of contemporary borders. In an ideal world, we would allow all people to participate freely in global circulation – but, politically, that's not realistic or sustainable in today's world. The rise of populist nationalism has caused a reassertion of 'sovereignty' and borders, and we've seen a backlash against migrants and refugees. A more realistic medium-term objective has to be to create a world of what I call 'sustainable migration', one in which we are able to support the rights of refugees, and people with human-rights-based claims to move, and then ensure that migration is managed in a way that can benefit all, migrants themselves, receiving societies and sending societies. The challenge of today and the immediate future is not to create a borderless world. It's to create a world of sustainable migration which is more inclusive of those who currently risk being left behind, whether citizens, refugees or migrants.

Catherine Woollard: We need to find a way to manage our borders in a way that respects human rights and allows those entitled to protection to cross. We are in a situation now where people's rights under international law are sometimes not respected, so people who need protection cannot move, and this leads to huge amounts of suffering. Europe is trying to export its migration panic and hence impose an unrealistic and damaging model of border control, whereas borders in reality are far more fluid and permeable. This anachronistic view of migration is having horrendous humanitarian consequences for the 66 million forcibly displaced people around the world, and Europe's move backwards towards treating the movement of people as a threat may have knock-on effects in other regions, and put people at further risk.

George Rupp: A borderless world would be feasible only if we treated people as individuals who are respected by the whole human community. This notion of atomistic individuals who can each one relate to a universal human community is often expressed in various iterations of modern Western individualism. But the unbridled individualism now evident in much of the West and especially in the United States fails to recognize that communities are also indispensable, that we are all members of communities, and that the capacity to embrace differences can be cultivated within communities. This goal of inclusive communities is admittedly also idealistic, but it is a more achievable goal than a borderless world. We need a richer culture that embraces the texture of human communities, and builds on it, rather than simply rejecting it.

There is a sense that war can never be justified. But as we know when we look back at history, while a fair society would perhaps not need war, society is not fair and circumstances emerge that are so painful, and so unjust, conflict seems unavoidable. We must be careful not to become desensitized to the brutality of war either. As Ben Ferencz told me during our interview, it's important to understand how unhelpful it is to glorify the act of war, notwithstanding our rightful celebration of the acts of bravery that occur within war.

War and conflict do not exist as natural phenomena apart from us. More than being instinctual, they are choices we actively make as a species against our own kind, largely driven by cultural, economic, political and social factors along with unbridled examples of self-interest, which not only have been created by us, but which could be largely avoided. As Bertie Ahern told me, armed conflict is indeed anathema to how the world should work, but it is something that often results out of issues that cannot be resolved by negotiation, or simply because parties have not put enough effort into conciliation and dialogue. Having experienced this first-hand through the conflict that played out in Ireland, Bertie is well placed to comment on this, and I was struck by the sadness he felt about the fact that the mechanisms of peacebuilding and conflict resolution often only come into play once wars are already underway. Research also shows how averse we as humans are to inflicting violence on our own kind and this is perhaps why, as Jody Williams explained, the tools used to get the masses to engage in war rest on creating differences to otherize the 'enemy' – to break the bonds of humanity, we must first deny it as existing in those who we want to conquer.

In today's world, we need to understand conflict more than ever. As Lech Wałęsa described it, we live in a world with growing populism where demagogues are gaining power on a massive scale. History has shown how easy it is for these groups to destroy society, and that is precisely why we need to find new structures to organize and unite us. We create a utopian vision of peace as being something in the future, an oasis visible on the horizon of the fog of conflict, but it is perhaps our own philosophy that means we cannot comprehend peace as existing in the present. We tend to define the value of morality in terms of evils that have been perpetrated and the value of tolerance by the hatred that has been levied. These modes of thinking are remnants of a history defined by war, conflict and its glorification – a mode of human development perhaps to be called 'adolescence'. In almost every way, however, humanity is now ready to progress from adolescence into adulthood. We have the technology, knowledge and infrastructure to genuinely create an egalitarian world, rich in opportunity and free of many of the scourges that have ravaged us for centuries.

Ben Ferencz investigated Nazi war crimes after the Second World War and was Chief Prosecutor for the United States at the Nuremberg Trials. More than most, he understands the causes and consequence of war. It was clear from my conversation with him that we need to find mechanisms to settle disputes, whatever they are, without war. He passionately spoke about our need to stop glorifying war, for it is hell. When I met Ben he was ninety-eight, and he acknowledged that it is no longer his fight, but for the young people of today's world there can be no greater call to action than to wake up, speak up and stop this love affair with war. Plato mused that 'only the dead have seen the end of war', but it will perhaps be the greatest victory of mankind to claim that vision for the living.

 # BIOGRAPHIES

Bertie Ahern retired as Taoiseach (Irish Prime Minister) in 2008, the first person in over sixty years to have been elected to that office on three successive occasions. He was instrumental in the negotiation of the historic Good Friday Agreement, a framework for power-sharing in Northern Ireland.

Martti Ahtisaari is a politician, Nobel Peace Prize laureate and United Nations diplomat. He was the tenth president of Finland from 1994 to 2000 and is noted for his work on international peace.

Professor Zeid Ra'ad Al Hussein is the Perry World House Professor of the Practice of Law and Human Rights at the University of Pennsylvania. He was the UN's sixth High Commissioner for Human Rights and has served as the President of the UN Security Council.

Professor Alexander Betts is a British political scientist. He is the Leopold Muller Professor of Forced Migration and International Affairs, a William Golding Senior Fellow in Politics at Brasenose College, and Associate Head of the Social Sciences Division at the University of Oxford.

Marina Cantacuzino is an award-winning British journalist and founder of The Forgiveness Project, a non-profit organization dedicated to exploring forgiveness and justice through stories.

THOUGHT ECONOMICS

Professor François Crépeau is a Canadian lawyer and Director of the McGill Centre for Human Rights and Legal Pluralism, and a professor at McGill University. His previous roles include time as a United Nations Special Rapporteur on the Human Rights of Migrants. He is a fellow of the Royal Society of Canada.

Dr Shirin Ebadi is an Iranian political activist, lawyer and human rights activist. She is the founder of the Defenders of Human Rights Centre in Iran. In 2003 she was awarded a Nobel Peace Prize for her activism, making her the first Iranian and first Muslim woman to receive one.

Ben Ferencz is an American lawyer. He was an investigator of Nazi war crimes after the Second World War and the Chief Prosecutor for the United States Army at one of the twelve military trials held at Nuremberg.

Gulwali Passarlay is an Afghan refugee, author, TEDx speaker, and a Politics major at the University of Manchester. He is the co-founder of My Bright Kite, which aims to empower young refugees, and a Global Youth Ambassador for Theirworld.

Professor George Rupp is an American theologian. He has held the positions of President of Rice University, Columbia University, and the International Rescue Committee. He has written numerous articles and published six books.

Lech Wałęsa is a statesman, Nobel Peace Prize laureate and former President of Poland. He was the first democratically elected president of the country and has received hundreds of honours, including over forty honorary degrees.

Jody Williams is an American political activist. In 1997 she was awarded the Nobel Peace Prize for her work on banning anti-personnel landmines. In addition, she has received fifteen honorary degrees and has been named by *Forbes* as one of the 100 most powerful women in the world.

Catherine Woollard is Director of the European Council on Refugees and Exiles, an alliance of 106 NGOs across forty European countries, whose mission is to protect and advance the rights of refugees, asylum-seekers and other forcibly displaced persons.

ON DEMOCRACY: A 2,500-YEAR EXPERIMENT IN POWER

'Democracy is not an aggregation, it's dialectical – it's a dialogue. Every time a conversation takes place, you emerge as a different person. Part of the other person has become part of you, and part of you has become part of the other person.'

YANIS VAROUFAKIS

It's 8 May 2020 as I write this, and German President Frank-Walter Steinmeier is giving a speech at the Central Memorial of the Federal Republic of Germany to the Victims of War and Tyranny (Neue Wache) to commemorate the seventy-fifth anniversary of the liberation of Germany from National Socialism, and the end of the Second World War in Europe. 'In 1945 we were liberated,' he says. 'Today, we must liberate ourselves from the temptations of a new brand of nationalism. From a fascination with authoritarianism. From distrust, isolationism and hostility between nations. From hatred and hate speech, from xenophobia and contempt for democracy – for they are but the old evil in a new guise.'

To understand the story of humanity is to bear witness to the story of its greatest paradox: power. This phenomenon creates the constraints in which we operate, yet is responsible for the structures that bind our society together. The exercise and accumulation of power is endemic to humanity. In the twentieth century alone, this phenomenon has been responsible for over 200 million deaths through war and oppression, and has concentrated over 50 per cent of the world's wealth into the hands of just 1 per cent of the world's population, meaning that billions of our global family have been subjected to hunger, thirst and disease. Power has also enabled social movements that have brought rights, freedoms and opportunity to many billions more.

For those of us living in occidental civilization, the deeper questions of how our society functions are largely delegated up the chain to (usually) elected leaders; the safety valve being that if we don't like them, we will (again, usually) vote in someone else who better suits our collective interests. In reality, whether we look at the United States of America, the United Kingdom, Kenya or India, today's democratic experiments often still cede control to the best-funded, most vocal, or emotive groups, and often leave out vast swathes of the population who may have suffrage, but no material benefit from it. The blasé relationship of the majority of Western citizens to democratic processes is perhaps because we've lived so long at peace, we've forgotten the price of it. And because we've forgotten the cost, we ignore the value – allowing political systems to emerge that give us a sense of participation optically, yet where power is still substantively concentrated out of the hands of the many, into the few.

In this chapter are excerpts of the conversations I've had with some of the most respected thinkers in the field to explore the very essence of democracy, and citizen participation in politics, such as Noam Chomsky, A. C. Grayling and Garry Kasparov, as well as those at the frontline of the fight for democracy, such as former Allied Commander of NATO, Admiral James Stavridis. For many of us, particularly in Europe and the USA, criticizing our leaders is almost a national pastime, yet of course the reality is that being in those positions of power is complex and challenging – especially when trying to balance the interests of an entire population. To learn more, I also spoke to the former prime minister of Belgium, Guy Verhofstadt, the former president of Estonia, Toomas Hendrik Ilves, and Vicente Fox Quesada, former president of Mexico.

What is democracy?

A. C. Grayling: The most general characterization of democracy is that suitably enfranchised people of voting age have the final say to confer authority on the government a state has. The way that franchised will is expressed differs from one system to another. Democracy allows an expression of popular will on the policies and parties that might form a government. We have a very unsatisfactory electoral system in the UK, but there is broad consensus to accept how it works. A referendum on proportional representation was rejected by the country a few years ago, so we stick with the 'first-past-the-post' system. For most of history, people have been worried that democracy too readily degenerates into ochlocracy (mob rule), and as a result, almost all democratic systems have structures and institutions in place to filter out the danger of a collapse into mob sentiment. There is a saying, generally attributed to Churchill, which is that 'the best argument against democracy is a five-minute conversation with the average voter'. People tend to be incompletely informed, too self-interested and too short-termist. The ideal democracy is one where people are very well informed and think of the good of all, not just themselves, and that's simply not what happens. In the UK, we have a representative democracy. The people sent to parliament are not merely messengers or delegates; they are sent in order to get the information, to do some thinking, to discuss, debate, make judgements and act on behalf of their constituents and the country as a whole. If we don't like what they do, we can chuck them out at the next election. While they are in parliament, these individuals are supposed to be acting on our behalf. We have what you might call a constitutional arrangement, a constitutional democracy, which is the right kind of compromise between mob rule at one extreme and autocracy and tyranny at the other.

Ted Lieu: Democracy, at a fundamental level, means that the people in a country decide the direction they want the country to go. It means following the rule of law and making sure that individuals have their rights protected. Those are the core principles of any democracy.

Bassem Youssef: Different people have different interpretations of democracy and most people who come to power through 'democratic' means think democracy is just the tyranny of a majority, and that's a problem. In the Middle East we see this tyrannical democracy with political and military leaders who feel they can do what they want if they have sufficient votes. I believe that democracy first and foremost is about the protection of minorities and those people in society who need help. For those who are already powerful or wealthy, democracy is meaningless. Democracy matters to those who need protection, and who may not otherwise be vindicated through the democratic process. With enough votes, you can change a country's constitution, you can put people in jail, you can start passing laws that would impact human rights. If you have a democracy that protects everyone, in all situations, that is a true democracy.

Why does democracy matter?

Garry Kasparov: If we look at human history, we can see a simple answer to the question of democracy. This system provides the best conditions for individuals and society to flourish. Most of the world's wealth has been produced by democratic countries, and while people may point to China and other countries where living standards are growing, the driving engine of innovation, which is the foundation of human progress, still sits in the heart of the free world. Free people are far more capable of realizing their potential.

To what extent are our societies free and democratic?

Noam Chomsky: These societies are quite free by historical standards. They are democratic in the sense that they have formal elections that aren't stolen, and so on. They're undemocratic to the extent that forces other than popular will have an overwhelming effect on who can participate in electoral outcomes. The United States is the most extreme in this respect. Right now in the United States, elections are essentially bought. You can't run an election unless you have a huge amount of capital, which means overwhelmingly, although not 100 per cent, that capital is sought from strong corporate backing. For example, in the 2008 election, what carried Obama across the finish line first was a very substantial amount of support from financial institutions which are now the core of the economy. The coming elections are supposed to be a 2-billion-dollar election, and there's only one place to go for that kind of money. There used to be a system of chairs of committees in Congress, who were there through seniority and so on. By now, it is generally required that funding go to the party committee, which means those are also, in large part, bought. This means that popular opinion is very much marginalized. You can see this very clearly on issue after issue. So, the huge issue right now, domestically, is the deficit. Well, people have ideas about how to get rid of the deficit. For example, most of the deficit is the result of a highly dysfunctional healthcare system which has about twice the per-capita cost of other countries and by no means better outcomes – in fact, rather poorer outcomes. The population has long favoured moving towards some kind of national healthcare system, which would be much less expensive and (judging by the outcomes) no worse – maybe better. That would, in fact, eliminate the deficit. That's not even considered.

Do citizens understand how government should relate to them?

Michael Lewis: In the United States, citizens have stopped thinking of themselves as citizens but have started thinking of themselves as customers, thus relieving themselves of any obligations whatsoever when it comes to understanding how government functions. Civics used to be part of the curriculum in American primary education, but vanished, and so you have a generation of people who simply don't know the nuances of how the process of government works and therefore will believe any lie, any slander about government. Without civics education, people simply will not have the knowledge or information they need to defend themselves from politicians who say X, Y or Z about government. For example, Rick Perry, Governor of Texas, wanted to eliminate three whole departments of government. Why? Because it's a guaranteed applause line. Guess what, he's now in charge of one of the departments he wanted to eliminate! The energy department which, among other things, tends to our nuclear arsenal. A lot of what I'm saying about Americans and their relationship to government will surely apply elsewhere in the world, and fundamentally we have a problem where people get all sorts of things from government but have little understanding or appreciation of where those things come from and rarely do they participate and give anything back.

Why are we seeing a surge in right-wing and populist movements?

Ece Temelkuran: The Second World War taught us a specific aesthetic of fascism. We always imagine that Nazi uniform, and the kind of futuristic authoritarian settings we see on Netflix and HBO. In our culture, we see the uniform and the militaristic as the representations of authoritarianism and fascism. Today, right-wing populism, authoritarianism and neo-fascism are coming from different places. Reality

TV stars, strange men, and people who otherwise would be considered national jokes. Many of today's right-wing populist leaders are political figures that nobody really took seriously from the beginning. Nobody expected that neo-fascism could take hold with swagger, in such a laid-back manner.

To understand why these phenomena are creeping back into our world, you have to look for the roots. Neoliberalism has, since the 1970s, imposed this idea that the free-market economy is the best and most ethical system humanity can come up with to organize itself. Neoliberalism changed the definition of what human fundamental morals are, and what justice means – and it's created a new kind of being. The neoliberalist model has been put forward as a solution to which there is no alternative; we've crippled the political spectrum, cut the left away, and shifted everything to the right. Politics has become a competition – who can be further right and who can further deliver numbing of the mind through consumerism. After all, people are only allowed to be free when they consume, and thus we are political objects, not political subjects. Politics has become entertainment and people feel like their opinions do not matter any more.

Vicente Fox: Politics is a pendulum; it swings from the left, to the right, to the left, to the right. You get into government and you see the liberals, the extreme left, populism, demagoguery. They don't work or convince, they mess up things, and then people look towards the right – the conservatives. There is no 'left or right' in this sense, it's just the way things develop. There are times you need conservatism to keep the fundamentals of the economy in line with disciplined approaches to growth and debt. And guess what, this creates jobs and wealth. At the same time this limits the budget and limits the possibilities for new ideas and new social programmes. People then go to the other side where you distribute income, come up with social programmes, and have social innovation. This is exactly what happened with Obama who, with the Democrats and liberals, went strongly towards the social responsibility side. But now, the conservatives are saying, 'No! No! It's too much! The debt is too high! We need to stop this nonsense and go back the other way!' – I think this is normal. We're never going to have a world with only one path and one philosophy. People change, economies change, the distribution of income changes, wealth changes, and then you have to adapt your political model and philosophy in the right direction.

Alastair Campbell: The right wing have always been better disciplined and better organized. You can look at UKIP and the Tories and argue they're a shambles, but they have better links into think tanks, the media and the business community. The right always has these in-built advantages. The left, the social democracies of Britain and America, seem to be ploughing a tough uphill furrow.

After the financial crisis of 2007/08, the assumption was that people would think capitalism didn't work, and thus would move more to the left. In fact, people decided the crisis was such a catastrophe that they had to look after themselves instead and they turned inwards. Just look at the extraordinarily toxic campaigns in the *Daily Mail*, such as their most recent one against foreign aid. They're saying to governments, 'Sod all these foreigners, sod foreign aid, sod community, just look after me.' People can appeal to the basic feelings of fear within us. We've seen it through history with Hitler and in the modern day with Farage, Le Pen, Trump and their peers. It's easy to play to fear, and not so easy to play to hope. In Europe, we've had twenty-five years of systematic misrepresentation by the right-wing media and politicians, and the public have been misled by it. As a result of this, people feel alienated from politics, and see the government as 'the establishment'. Don't forget though, it's not always the right wing who become the anti-establishment voice. Just look at Greece and Spain, and more recently here in the UK, Jeremy Corbyn. This is not about right and left wing, but rather anti-establishment versus establishment, populism versus elites.

A. C. Grayling: Today's politics shows the first-past-the-post system's imperfections. When we had a coalition government before 2015, the coalition partners were able to restrain the major parties and so policies tended to be more sensible and centre road. With our first-past-the-post system, a one-person majority in the Commons can completely override all our constitutional provisions, and that's bad. At the moment, we have a government which has been hijacked by its own right wing, and we're seeing things go off course. The system we now have of party 'whips' and loyalty is a challenge. If we had MPs who were not under the control of a party 'machine', it is unlikely we would see the more extreme measures that a far-left or far-right party would create should they have a majority. If you look at our history since the Second World War, we haven't seen the choice of more extreme leaders that we are seeing now. Characters like Trump, Farage and Le Pen have always been there, occupying an extreme, minority position on the fringe of the political spectrum.

A combination of recent factors has given them the opportunity to come to the forefront. The 2007 financial meltdown caused many middle- and low-class working people to get 'stuck' economically; their position hasn't improved greatly since 2008 and, in fact, for many, things have got worse. People at the top end of the scale, however, have continued to get richer. This toxic increasing inequality is an extremely dangerous political beast. In the European and American context, immigration has become a problem word. In too many ways, the word immigration has become a way to conceal xenophobia and even racism. I'm afraid we've seen expressions of that in the UK, USA and in Europe throughout recent political campaigns. The implosion of the Middle East has created floods of refugees who are escaping places of conflict and strife, placing great pressure on the EU. Just look at the boat people going to Italy and migrants travelling to Greece and the Balkans. This has inflamed the anti-immigration sentiment. Immigration and the stagnation of economic possibilities for those a little lower down the economic scale have given populism its moment. People like Farage, Trump and Le Pen have captured this and run with it.

Guy Verhofstadt: There has been an increase of populist and nationalist movements recently, but that does not mean it cannot be stopped. In order to stop this movement, we need to understand what caused it. Populist politicians are quick to promise solutions to everyone's problems, with so-called 'simple solutions'. People who have not seen the benefits of globalization, and who feel disenfranchised and ignored, see these populists offering a quick fix and place their faith in them. However, these populist politicians rarely deliver. Just look at the Brexit vote in the UK. In the weeks after the vote, the politicians who campaigned for leave started going back on their promises, such as the infamous £350 million a week for the NHS. Trump is the same. He has already started reneging on the promises he made in the election campaign when he realized he cannot deliver them. With the rise of populist politicians and the growth of nationalism, politics in Europe is no longer a fight between the left and the right. It is increasingly a conflict between those who fight for open societies and those who want to see closed societies. Yet this increased support for authoritarian and Eurosceptic far-right parties, combined with dramatic falls in democratic engagement, should worry all of us.

Defeating nationalism and populism means addressing the concerns of those left behind by globalization and dispelling the myths of a quick fix. For me, the solution is to manage globalization in a fairer way, not to build walls and retreat to nationalism in the hope that this will deliver prosperity, improve security or deliver fairer societies – it won't. We also need to streamline our political institutions and increase transparency in public institutions. We must listen to people's concerns about globalization, but the response should not be protectionism, but rather to shape globalization so that it works for us. The European Union has the power to shape globalization and we should harness it. We need to listen to people's concerns, not sneer at them, and offer a radical new vision for effective governance. Otherwise, nationalism will spread further.

Ted Lieu: In the United States, even before the 2016 election, it was clear we had two economies in our nation. If you have a college degree or higher, you're probably doing OK or quite well; you might be in the technology, healthcare, aerospace or financial sectors. If you have a high-school degree or less, the last two decades will have been a disaster for you. You will be angry, you will want to make things better, but in your mind the system is failing you. So then, come the election, and Bernie Sanders, who is not even a Democrat, almost won the Democratic primary. How does that happen? Because he tapped into a lot of that anger and directed it at the billionaires on Wall Street. He almost won. Donald Trump happened to tap into even more anger, and he decided to direct it at immigrants and minorities, and he did win. Donald Trump has not actually been able to address their concerns. He has not been able to bring back jobs – in fact, companies are shedding workers in many sectors relevant to his base. These are very hard issues, and a lot of it is connected with automation and a changing economy. But it's hard to blame robots, so Donald blamed minorities and immigrants; even though people know it's not true, they needed someone to blame. It was very clear to me, for a pretty long time, that for a large part of America this system was not working – and people were angry. They wanted to make changes and blow up the system.

Ece Temelkuran: People sometimes look to the Middle East to see where things are going wrong, but I must say, in Turkey, perhaps our democracy was stronger – it took decades for Erdoğan to achieve what Boris Johnson did in a few weeks. Maybe we had a better resistance. I have to say though, it's difficult to find something positive to say about the fight against authoritarianism in the Middle East, but I am incredibly inspired by the fight of young women in Turkey and the Middle East – fighting for democracy with their lives. They are unstoppable. When it comes to Europe and the Western democracies, we have to take to the streets and make ourselves heard – end of story. We have to organize, mobilize and politicize. We have to use those good old-fashioned tools of politics – they're the ones that count. We have to show up! We have to fight, we have to get out onto the streets and change things. Since the 1970s it's almost become a taboo to talk of conflict. We've become a society geared around consensus and co-existence – and this has domesticated politics in a dangerous way. The media have been too busy finding consensus with the Brexiters and Trumpeters to fight them; this is a political struggle and there is no politeness or kindness in it. It is very clear what one has to do if one has to defend their rights – you have to fight back when there is oppression.

The philosopher Jean-Pierre Faye posited that rather than being opposite and opposing ends of the political continuum, the far-left and far-right resemble one another as manifestations of populism. Over the past decade, I have travelled around the world with In Place of War, a charity that works in places of conflict. The sheer magnitude of economic and social injustice around the world, combined with the forces of climate change, corruption and foreign policy, are creating environments where people have lost hope. This manifests in anger, in a pushback against the system, and often creates the conditions for populism to flourish. It is not a fallacy to describe our world as zero-sum. The gains of occidental civilization have come at a huge cost to the rest of humanity, and the mechanisms of this approach are deeply embedded in our foreign policy.

What really drives our foreign policy and how does that impact on us as citizens?

Noam Chomsky: Foreign policy in the UK and Europe tends to follow the United States – not entirely, but the US does remain the prime driver in foreign policy. It's not a secret what foreign policy is driven by. For example, Bill Clinton was quite explicit about it. His position, expressed clearly in Congress, was that the US has the right to carry out a unilateral military action, sometimes supported by a so-called 'coalition of the willing' in order to secure resources and markets, and it must have military forces forward deployed, meaning foreign bases in Europe and elsewhere, in order to shape events in our interest. Our interest does not mean the American people, but rather the interests of those who design policy, primarily the corporate sector.

Foreign policy can be undertaken in ways which are expected to harm security. In fact, that's not at all uncommon. If you follow the Chilcot inquiry, the head of MI5 testified, merely extending what was already known, but she testified that both the United States and Britain recognized that Saddam Hussein was not a threat and that the invasion would very likely increase the threat of terror. And, in fact, it did! About seven-fold in the first year according to quasi-governmental statistics. So an invasion was undertaken that would harm the citizens of the invading countries, as indeed it did. At first, of course, the reasons were presented with the usual boilerplate, which is informative presentation that goes along with every act of force, citing democracy and all sorts of wonderful things.

When it was becoming clear that the war's end could not be easily achieved, towards the end of the invasion certain policies were stated clearly. In November 2007, the Bush administration issued a declaration of principles stating that any agreement with Iraq would have to ensure the unlimited ability of US forces to operate there – essentially permanent military bases – and such an agreement would also secure the privileging of US investors in the energy systems. In 2008, Bush reiterated and, in fact, strengthened this in a message to Congress where he said that he would ignore any legislation that limits US capacity to use force in Iraq or that interferes with US control over Iraqi oil. That was stated very clearly and explicitly. In fact, the US had to back down from this goal as a result of Iraqi resistance, but the goals themselves were clear and explicit and had nothing to do with the security of Americans. The same is true elsewhere; so, one leading specialist on Pakistan recently reviewed US policies in Afghanistan and Pakistan, revealing once again that these policies are significantly increasing the threat of terror and in fact possibly nuclear terror. He concluded that American and British soldiers are dying in Afghanistan in order to make the world less secure for Americans and British. That's not so unusual. Security is not, typically, a very top priority of states. There are other interests.

Why is anti-European sentiment growing?

Toomas Hendrik Ilves: People are always dissatisfied with the status quo. It's kind of a gut reaction, but I think if you were rationally trying to think about going it alone, those who are anti-European would have considerable difficulty in rationally making a case for doing it. Smaller countries would struggle to do well economically or even from a security perspective outside Europe in these times. They would be subject to all kinds of bullying. One reason why Russia particularly despises the European Union is their preference for bilateral relationships. However, the bilateral relationships they could and would build would be completely domineering, even with Europe's largest member state, Germany – and that doesn't even take into account smaller countries on the periphery where Russia may even have had an interest. We are seeing lots of strong atavistic emotional responses in Europe – we certainly saw it during the French election – but I don't know how atavistic the people of France would continue to be if their economy went south and they needed visas to travel to their neighbouring countries like Spain and Germany.

Are referendums an essential part of democracy?

Alastair Campbell: You have to see things in a historical context. If you live in Switzerland, for example, there is a commitment to public consultation and decision by referendum. This seems to work for them. One of our strengths, and one of the things often admired about Britain, is that we're a parliamentary democracy. There are faults in any political system, but ours has done pretty well, partly because of constituency representation that gives people a local representative in government, and partly because we choose the government who make decisions on our behalf. The weakness of Cameron's referendum strategy was that he wasn't doing it as a means of taking forward his strategy for the UK in Europe, but rather that he was using it as a tactic to shut up UKIP and the Tory right. The populists and right-wing press would jump on any attempt to not permit a vote on such topics as being tantamount to saying, 'You don't trust the public.' This is not about trusting or not trusting the public; it's about the fact that we, as a population, make a decision about choosing the people who govern us, and we also reserve the right to get rid of those people if they don't do their job. I think referendums are very dangerous.

It is thought that Charles de Gaulle once said, 'Politics is too serious a matter to be left to the politicians.' Of course, politics is not only a serious business, but also a complex one. The gravity of governance is such that the level of information required to make decisions is practically impossible for any single individual or small group to fathom. While referenda may work for small, relatively predictable groups, for countries and continents in a globalized world they will give you nothing more than an emotional temperature reading, rather than a strategic output. This is arguably why the absence of any real civics education in Western curricula is so dangerous.

Do we need to get more involved in political discourse?

Vicente Fox: We need to have much more citizen involvement in politics; much more educated involvement. I am very disappointed with Brexit, for instance, where people who went to vote did not represent the whole constituency of citizens, and did not represent specifically the future. The young were not there. The Brexit campaign was run by populists who did not know what Brexit meant, and who were not informing citizens about the losses that Britain's economy would face.

They were only siding with nationalism, and misinforming voters about what the country needed from this referendum. Trump, this crazy guy, campaigned around a referendum. He asked people, 'What do you want to have? A strong successful America? Or an America that has failed under the Obama administration?' That's a false debate; it was a trap. Trump is a false prophet who has the capacity to speak and convince people around the wrong ideas. Electors have to prepare themselves much better. They have to read and get the information they need to make the right decisions. Today's democracies are not delivering. Today's democracies are presenting false alternatives. These messianic leaders, these false prophets, are taking people to the land of nowhere, taking people to the desert. It's very dangerous.

What are the consequences of a lack of public engagement and public knowledge around their own democracy?

Guy Verhofstadt: A lack of public engagement and the public feeling disenfranchised is a key issue facing the European Union. We need to make our democratic institutions more transparent and accountable in order to make citizens more invested and interested in these institutions. Public knowledge is very important too, and more transparency can make it easier for the public to have more knowledge about their democratic institutions. It has been evident from the Brexit vote and following discussions since the vote in the UK that there was a lack of understanding about the European Union and how it works. Phrases like sovereignty were used a lot throughout the campaign, but when the case was taken to court as to whether the UK parliament should have a vote on triggering Article 50, there was outrage among some leave voters. Ostensibly, this was what they supposedly wanted back: parliamentary sovereignty. So it is very important that the citizens feel involved in politics and that they have a good knowledge of their democracy, because otherwise people can feel cheated by decisions made, or feel disenfranchised, and therefore don't participate in their democracy.

What will it take to re-engage society with government?

Michael Lewis: I think it's going to take people being genuinely terrified before they really respond to the crisis of lack of political engagement. I fear we're going to have to experience a national disaster – maybe a virus, maybe a war, or maybe something like a financial crisis or depression. It may take something that severe to stimulate civic re-engagement.

People often don't care about how their car or computer works until it breaks; those with a working knowledge of mechanics or electronics can get their toolkit out and get to work. But for the majority, they are opening a black box – the access to which is controlled by mechanics and technicians as expensive gatekeepers. Politics is no different. The majority of people don't care about it, until it breaks. The Brexit referendum in Britain spurred a whole generation, dismayed at the result, into political action, and the Covid-19 pandemic showed the real value of global political cooperation, and the downsides to isolationism in a hyperconnected world.

What is power?

Moisés Naím: The classical definition of power, commonly used by political scientists and others, is that power is the capacity to get others to do or stop doing something now, or in the future. Power is also a source of order, and a source of comfort for some people. Remember that the extreme situation, where nobody has power, is anarchy, and anarchy is an inferior Hobbesian society, which leads to inferior social outcomes to societies where structures and entities that impose power, limits and rules create stability and prosperity. Some neuroscientists have even argued that power is hard wired into our brains, and evolutionary psychologists have similarly argued that power and the quest for it is an evolutionary trait, an instinct.

Admiral James Stavridis: There are several centres of power that drive society in a broad sense. First and foremost, we see demographics – human capital, the people and population – tied to which we see their education levels and productivity. Traditionally, we also talk of military power, albeit I think this is suffering from the law of diminishing terms as, in our current global society, huge force-on-force confrontations are less likely, though not impossible. Increasingly, cyber or information power is also extremely significant, and I would tie this to the concept of 'idea' or 'message' power, which is society's ability to influence other parts of the world in the power of its messages. I would argue that Western society, over the past several centuries, has been able to move the ideas of democracy, freedom of speech, freedom of education, freedom of assembly, gender rights, racial equality and more. Given that the centre of power can be seen as your ability to produce or convey influential ideas, this is certainly important. Cultural power is also significant, the degree to which your society's popular culture – films, books, art, theatre, music and sports – is received nationally and internationally. Separate from this is political power, which, in many ways, derives from all the other things I've spoken about. Geographic and resource power are also fundamentally important, and are derived from not just the size of your country, but from how much water and energy you have access to. Innovation power is also very important – the creative spark your society has. All these factors taken together will determine how influential a nation is at influencing the behaviours of other nations and organizations.

Do citizens understand the influence of power in their lives?

Moisés Naím: Increasingly, broader populations are aware of the impact power plays in their lives. There is so much to applaud in the trends we are seeing. This is a world with more opportunity, and where those who have been excluded and disempowered can shape their own futures and change their conditions. This is a world where authoritarians have a hard time holding on to power, and where those who want to create a political movement, a company, a religion or NGO have a chance to do so. I'm not saying that power concentrations do not exist. There are countries, companies and individuals who continue to possess immense power. From Vladimir Putin to the Head of Goldman Sachs, and from the editor of the *New York Times* to the head of Google, and even China's leader or Pope Francis, the Vatican, Pentagon, Kremlin and even Mountain View (the headquarters of Google) – these are all immense centres of global power. All of these centres do, however, have a harder time wielding and retaining their power. Their ability to perpetuate power is significantly less than in the past.

Admiral James Stavridis: The vast majority of our citizens enjoy their lives, face the challenges of the world, struggle or are entertained by what happens, are occasionally threatened by it or, if they're unfortunate to live somewhere like Syria, they will feel it very extremely and tragically. Most people, however, do not spend time focused on these larger questions. Leadership matters. In a democracy, we select somebody to worry about the big problems for us. We criticize them, support them and maybe tire of them and throw them out of office. We, as a people, do not spend an inordinate amount of time worrying about big problems; we outsource that to our leaders and use tools to shape the outcomes for our country.

Democracy has a better chance overall of being the long-term solution; it creates a safety valve. If you don't have democracy, if you don't elect a leader and put some of your skin in the game, the pressures build up, and this is what we're seeing in China right now. People there do not have a say in the election of their leaders, and while they were content when growth was in double-digits, when that growth slows and leaves debt, environmental damage, inequality and corruption, they are found without a safety valve. This can play out very broadly in a society where there is no buy-in with a system like democracy. While the Chinese may argue the counter and say that democracy is messy and cannot be used to make decisions, I would point them to Winston Churchill, who said, 'Democracy is the worst system of government, except for everything else.' Power is more diffused in democracy, and that allows those at the centre to let go a little bit and allow power to be more equally shared through the population.

What influence do large corporations exert in society?

Noam Chomsky: Corporations play an overwhelming role in society. I don't think that fact is even contentious. Similar observations have been made as far back as Adam Smith, who pointed out that in Britain the principal architects of policy were merchants and manufacturers, the people who own society, and they ensure that their interests are served however grievous the impact on the people of England. This is far more true today – with much higher concentrations of power, we are not just manufacturers, we have financial institutions and multinational corporations. They have an enormous influence, and the influence can not only be harmful, but in many cases lethal.

Taking the United States as an example, the corporate sector has been carrying out major propaganda campaigns to try to convince the population that there is no threat from global warming. This, in effect, has led to the majority of people now agreeing it is not a real issue. Business funding has also been the primary instrument in bringing a new group of cadres to Congress, figures who are virtually all climate-change deniers. These individuals are about to enact legislation to cut back funding for the international organization (the IPCC) and the capacity of the Environmental Protection Agency, who may not even be able to monitor the effect of greenhouse gases or carry out any other actions that could reduce the impact of global warming, which is a very serious threat. This has been done by the corporate executives who are carrying out these propaganda campaigns and fund political figures who undermine such efforts. They understand as well as anyone else that global warming is a very serious threat, but there is an institutional role that enters here. If you are the CEO of a corporation, your task is to maximize short-term profit. That's much more true now than it ever has been in the past. We are in a new stage of state capitalism in which the future just doesn't matter very much, even the survival of the firm doesn't matter very much. What matters increasingly is short-term profit and if a CEO doesn't pursue that, he will be replaced with someone who will do it. This is institutional effect, not individual effect, and has extraordinary implications for society. It may, in fact, destroy our very existence.

What is the role of law in the concept of democracy?

Lord Woolf: The law also provides the framework in which a democracy works. Democracy is, to those who are elected by the vote, an opportunity to make laws, subject to certain safeguards. Laws are essential for democracy to work effectively as much as the concept of democracy itself is committed to the rule of law. To this extent, I would say that there are some societies that work quite well even when their democratic processes are quite weak, as long as there are well-established processes for upholding the rule of law. I don't think democracy works at all well without even superficially recognizing the rule of law. For me, a terrorist organization that is democratically elected, for example, is just as flawed as a terrorist organization that is not elected. There are many examples of that. I see part of democracy as involving the values which are reflected by the rule of law.

Susan Herman: A couple of weeks ago, I happened to be visiting the Gettysburg battlefield and one thing which rings in my head are the words of Abraham Lincoln, who stated that government should be 'of the people, by the people, for the people'. That, to me, is the central idea of law in the concept of democracy. First, that laws should be by the people and of the people and for the people, and when you overlay on that the concept of justice (which paradoxically is a separate concept, though it should be inseparable), that the laws are going to be fairly executed and implemented. That is the role of law in a constitutional democracy and it is a step beyond the purpose of law in society.

I find that when I speak about the constitution, and some of the things the ACLU is working on, particularly in the United States, people are surprised when I tell them that we don't really live in a democracy. We live in a constitutional democracy. It's not true that what the majority of people want to do can be put into law because the constitution defines and sets aside certain principles (priori agreements) of who we want to be as a society. The rule of law then means that if a majority of people can get a law passed, that law is nevertheless invalid if it infringes on those fundamental principles. I think that is a very important element of justice, and I think it's very important in terms of law, not just in democracy, but in constitutional democracy. You can have a democracy that is not just, you can have laws that are not just, so the point of justice in this context requires something like a constitution, or something else that can take certain values or principles and states that no matter what the majority wants to do, these principles come first and trump everything else. That, to me, distinguishes between the rule of law and the rule of a mob.

When faced by threats such as terrorism, how can a nation balance the need for freedom with the need for security?

Lord Woolf: Lines have to be drawn. We have institutions who can authoritatively draw those lines and indicate where you must not go. We have a combination of values which are paramount – for example, the value which forbids torture in any circumstances. There are no grey areas, you just don't torture! At the same time, you have to have a protection of citizens. This is, arguably, the first role of government: to protect its citizens. So far as you can only keep that value to a limited extent, you must, using your resources, make up for any weakness in those very resources. Looking at increased government powers in monitoring of communications, I believe that has to be the position. We live in a society where we need to curtail rights so as to be able to protect the rights of our members of society. This is another area where drawing lines is important, but very difficult.

Susan Herman: I think the first answer is: with difficulty! Right after 9/11, people were very panicky about what had happened, and the temptation was to surrender some of our fundamental principles in the hope of becoming safer. There were a number of different things which happened in the United States. People talk of Guantanamo, a headline incursion on our principles of due process. The idea that you could just lock people up indefinitely with no hearing to determine whether or not they were really enemy combatants? I think that was a tremendous deviation from due process. And in that area, the Supreme Court was somewhat helpful, and we have had, at least, some hearings. I don't think they are, perhaps, as careful as they should be, but it's a start. We also gave up on a lot of liberties because of the temptation of Congress and the president to set up all sorts of dragnets; the idea that you have to do extensive surveillance and have all sorts of information in data banks because maybe you will be able to catch a terrorist that you would not otherwise be able to catch. And you have to therefore have criminal laws that have few defences, without much burden of proof required for the government because maybe then you will be able to catch a terrorist you wouldn't otherwise be able to catch.

We all know, however, that when you lay out dragnets, you also catch the unintended, and the First Amendment freedoms of speech, association and religion have all suffered because of the criminal laws and surveillance that we have been tempted into allowing. Post 9/11, the government also became much less transparent. They developed the 'mosaic theory' that any little piece of information about how we were combating terrorism, about what kind of surveillance we were doing, and how it was operating, was dangerous because, if the enemy were to combine that little piece of information with other little pieces of information, that might be helpful to them. They could adapt, and therefore the presumption was to not tell anyone anything, to keep it all secret. That lack of transparency became an enormous problem.

For a democratic society to work it requires a political system, a rule of law, human rights and the participation of people. Since the advent of modern democracy, which has been traced back to seventeenth-century England and the Petition of Right in 1628, there has been a natural tug of war between 'power' and 'people' over the extent to which a political system intervenes in civic society, the nature of law and its application, and to what extent those human rights are respected and defended. Phenomena like terrorism, and even the 2020 coronavirus pandemic, create a struggle for power between these pillars, but the participation element is critical as, without civic participation, there is no pushback against the mechanisms of power.

What would be your advice to the next generation?

Bassem Youssef: You have to question everything and bring everything out in the open. You cannot let anyone tell you what to think. Questioning is the one thing that scares everyone and scares power. Whether you ask your questions through debate, through comedy or through satire, question everything. Questioning is the prequel of the revolution.

Garry Kasparov: More and more young people are getting interested in politics, and we should praise Trump for waking them up. Democracy is not something that is granted for ever. Ronald Reagan once said, 'Freedom is never more than one generation away from extinction,' and our democratic instruments have got rusty, as people assumed they would always work automatically. The Trump victory demonstrated that many traditional pillars of democracy, such as avoiding conflict of interest and separating power, are in danger. The only solution to stopping this decline is to engage in politics. Look at the chaos being spread around the world by Trump's total incompetence, just in the first few months of his presidency. It is perhaps this chaos that has woken voters up to fight back against the rise of populism. Trump isn't intelligent enough to drive populism, but his inner circle, people like Steve Bannon, point out existing problems. Whether you talk about Farage, Le Pen or Bannon, they point out existing problems, saying the current government cannot run the country. Their solutions, however, will only ever make the situation much worse. It's very important to have an educated debate around democracy.

Yanis Varoufakis: I don't believe in giving advice – our generation did really badly! There can be no technical solution to working out what is in our common interests. We do not lack the technology to understand our society. Democracy is not an aggregation, it's dialectical – it's a dialogue. Every time a conversation takes place, you emerge as a different person. Part of the other person has become part of you, and part of you has become part of the other person. Democracy is not just about voting and aggregating, it's about reflecting into each other's thoughts, passions and ideas. We need to make that something we enjoy for its own sake. As Lenin used to say, in the end what matters is who does what to whom. It's all about power, and about overcoming. Politics is the overcoming of power relations.

Vicente Fox: You need to get involved in politics, profoundly involved. You need to commit with your nation and country to create a government that works. You need to be innovative. We need Einsteins, Newtons – we need people who don't believe in the established ideas but who create new things. Right now, the future of democracy is like an embryo. We are going to see the birth of new democratic structures, new ways of forming governments, new ways of forming parliaments and congresses. What we have today is not working and we need to invent new political parties. We need truth in our democracies and leaders who speak the truth. There is a lot of misleading, cheating and lies in public life today. You have to be frank, committed and inventive. Let's create a new world of truth, a world of institutions that are not corrupt, and a world of democratic institutions that work.

Guy Verhofstadt: It is important to remember that the crises of our time cannot be solved by a state on its own. The economic crisis, the refugee crisis, the fight against terrorism. Only by working together will we be able to tackle these problems and create a better world. Nationalism cannot be the answer, and if the trend towards nationalism continues, I would urge the younger generation to study the history of nationalism in Europe. It is not something we want to go back to. Having said that, I believe that, ultimately, nationalism will be rejected by future generations because its politicians are incapable of resolving the challenges we face, since they are global challenges. So my message to the next generation would be: learn about different cultures and build upon the values you share to work towards global solutions to global problems.

Democracy is not new; our world has been experimenting with it for over two and a half thousand years – but the current iteration of human civilization is the first where democracy has acquired a majority status when looking at how power is managed and distributed. The crises of democracy in our world are rather more about the quality of the democracy that is applied, as opposed to the quantity of democracy that exists. Examples of this are numerous, ranging from the dubious judicial legitimacy of elections to the manipulation of evidence that takes nations into war. From Trump to Modi, our world seems to feature an increasing number of pseudo-democratic authoritarians who repress those who challenge them, while giving everyone else just enough freedom to believe they are indeed free.

Bassem Youssef experienced first-hand the consequences of this, having to flee his country, Egypt, for criticizing government through his comedy and satire. In his view, democracy is first and foremost about protecting minorities and those who need help, and this makes sense. Democracy connects us to the notion of it being a pillar of equality. As Bassem told me, you simply cannot claim to have a democracy in any meaningful sense unless it protects everyone, in all situations. Even in our liberal Western democracy, we cannot be blind to this reality. In the ostensibly 'free' world, democratic overstep, including mass surveillance, shows that the extent to which our society is free and democratic is relative – we may have the appearance of freedom and democracy through our ability to vote and choose our leaders, but it isn't true democracy.

This view of being sufficiently free brings us back to the view of democracy being a compromise designed to balance interests among members of a community, although rather than balancing interests in a true sense, democracy as we see it becomes a pseudo-negotiation between a ruling elite –

be they political or corporate – and their peoples as to what freedoms they are prepared to cede in exchange for perceived comforts. This moral equilibrium point is further provoked into volatility by the huge inequality we see between societies, with the population of one wishing for the freedoms – be they economic, social, or political – in another. In Western civilization, consumerism has provided a unique substrate for this pact. People in all countries have found a way to disengage from the political process while living in comfort. Consumerism has provided the ultimate anaesthetic for the brain.

Unlike in true dictatorships, citizens in the West have a sense of debate, control and participation in the issues affecting their lives. This sense of participation is supported by the level of information citizens receive about their democracy and the opportunities they have to interact with it through voting rights, panels, protest and many other means. If, therefore, they feel sufficiently engaged in the democratic process, why should they even question the democracy of it? The fact is we are encountering what can only be described as a participation fallacy. Yes, citizens have the right to elect leaders – albeit ones who have sufficient capital to run for election – and vote on a wide variety of issues, but if we consider the most important issues that have had the most profound influence on Western society in the past decade, including wars, bank bailouts, climate change and more, aside from the right to show public opinion through protest, have citizens really had the opportunity to exercise public opinion? I believe the answer is no, and even the most cursory glance at public opinion polls and outlets will show the widespread displeasure at many decisions that, while ostensibly taken in citizens' best interests, rarely were.

This is not a problem we can solve overnight. The status quo has become embedded and systemic in every part of our society. For our world to truly become democratic, the process has to begin with education and end with culture, meaning that citizens are not only more aware of the opportunities and processes of democracy, but are also driven towards a culture that values tolerance, peace, prosperity and human dignity rather than one that prizes ignorance and dogma. Guy Verhofstadt was the forty-seventh prime minister of Belgium, and has been the European Parliament's Brexit coordinator since 2016, placing him at the centre of the largest crisis faced by Europe in peacetime. He told me how states cannot solve the crises we face on their own, and whether we consider the economic crises of our time our refugee crisis, or even the fight against terrorism, both will require all of us to work together. And he made clear how important it is that today's young people read history and understand that the return to nationalism we are seeing in Europe has potentially grave consequences.

'People, in the long run', stated David Eisenhower, 'are going to do more to promote peace than our governments. Indeed, I think that people want peace so much that one of these days governments had better get out of the way and let them have it.' For that to happen, though, we need to understand that we are in this together and that the notions of society and self-interest are, for the most part, incompatible. By understanding that in exchange for a few notional comforts we actively give up our own freedom and the freedoms of billions of citizens around the world, we lose any perceived moral high ground we have and any assertion of the freedom of our society.

 **BIOGRAPHIES**

Alastair Campbell is a British journalist, broadcaster, political aide and author. He held several positions in Downing Street, including Downing Street Director of Communications and spokesman for the Labour Party.

Noam Chomsky is an American linguist, philosopher, cognitive scientist, historian and political activist. He is both Institute Professor Emeritus at the Massachusetts Institute of Technology and Laureate Professor at the University of Arizona. He has written over a hundred books and received many honours, including the US Peace Prize.

Vicente Fox Quesada is a Mexican politician and businessman, and was the fifty-fifth President of Mexico. Since the end of his presidency he has been involved in the development of the Vicente Fox Centre of Studies, Library and Museum.

Professor A. C. Grayling is a British philosopher and author, and Master of the New College of the Humanities, and a Supernumerary Fellow of St Anne's College, Oxford.

Susan Herman is an American law scholar. She is the president of the American Civil Liberties Union and has taught at Brooklyn Law School since 1980.

Toomas Hendrik Ilves is a politician who served as the fourth President of Estonia from 2006 until 2016. Before that he worked as a diplomat and journalist, and leader of the Social Democratic Party.

Garry Kasparov is a Russian chess grandmaster, writer and political activist. Since retiring from chess, he has focused on writing and political activism, opposing the policies of Vladimir Putin.

Michael Lewis is the bestselling author of *The Undoing Project, Liar's Poker, Flash Boys, Moneyball, The Blind Side, Home Game* and *The Big Short*, among other works.

Ted Lieu is an American politician serving as the US Representative for California's thirty-third congressional district since 2015. He served in the US Air Force Judge Advocate General's Corps and since 2000 has served in the Air Force Reserve Command.

Moisés Naím is a Venezuelan journalist and writer. He was the former Minister of Trade and Industry for Venezuela, and Executive Director of the World Bank. Since 2012, he has directed and hosted a weekly televised news programme, *Efecto Naím*. He is a Distinguished Fellow at the Carnegie Endowment for International Peace.

Admiral James Stavridis is a retired United States Navy admiral. He currently holds many positions, including Operating Executive with The Carlyle Group and Chair of the Board of Counsellors at McLarty Associates.

Ece Temelkuran is a Turkish journalist, author and presenter. She is a former columnist for the widely read Turkish newspapers *Milliyet* and *Habertürk*. She was fired from *Habertürk* for writing articles that criticized the Turkish government.

Yanis Varoufakis is a Greek economist, academic, philosopher and politician. He is a former finance minister for the Greek government and is the founder and Secretary General of the left-wing political party MeRA25. He is the author of several books and in 2018 he launched Progressive International with US senator Bernie Sanders.

Guy Verhofstadt is a Belgian politician and was the forty-seventh Prime Minister of Belgium from 1998 to 2008. He was Deputy Prime Minister and Minister of Budget from 1985 to 1992 and has been an MEP for Belgium since 2009.

Lord Woolf (Harry Kenneth Woolf) is a British life peer and retired barrister and judge. He previously held roles including Master of the Rolls, Lord Chief Justice of England and Wales, and President of the Courts of England and Wales. He is a cross-bencher in the House of Lords.

Bassem Youssef is an Egyptian comedian, writer, producer, surgeon and television host. He hosted a satirical news programme inspired by *The Daily Show*, *El-Benameg*, from 2011 to 2014. In 2013, *Time* magazine named him as one of their 100 most influential people in the world.

INDEX

[Interviewee names in italics.]

A

Abramović, Marina 47
  can every life have meaning 30
  why art exists 41
activism 98, 170
  and art 201–2, 232
  why we need it 200–1
Adorno, Theodor 204
adversity, learning from 116–17
advertising 80–1
Afghanistan 255
Africapitalism 149–50
Agricultural Revolution 27, 46
Ahern, Bertie 208, 235, 237
  applying peacebuilding techniques
    222–3
  start of the peacebuilding process
    218
  on conflict in society 211
Ahtisaari, Martti 237
  on conflict as part of human
    nature 213
  is conflict ever justifiable 214–15
  message to the next generation 225
  possibility of world peace 223–4
  start of the peacebuilding process
    217–18
  on conflict in society 210
Al Hussein, Zeid Ra'ad 237
  creating resilient peace 219
  fragility of global order 215–16
  why peace breaks down 211–12
Al-Khalili, Jim 47
  philosophical implications of
    quantum mechanics 36
Aldrin, Buzz 15–16
Amazon 129
American Revolution 56
Amin Dada, Idi 208
Amoruso, Sophia 164
  separating facets of your identity
    146–7

anarchy 260
Ancelotti, Carlo 124
  building high-performance teams
    101
  how to build trust 103
  style of leadership needed today 97
  meaning of success and failure 110
  what it means to be a leader 96
Angelou, Maya 51, 86, 88
  role of poetry in our culture 59
  role of storytelling in our culture
    58
  what makes great writing 61
  why we write 54
  writing and ethical / social
    responsibility 65
  writing and other forms of culture
    62
  writing and social change 55–6
  written word and youth culture 64
animals 46
  Balinese monkey chants 67–8
  chimpanzees and great apes 39–40
  consciousness 38–9
Annan, Kofi 195–6
anti-European sentiment, growth of
  255–6
anti-Semitism 177, 199
  see also Holocaust
anxiety and depression see depression
  and anxiety
AOL 129, 141
apartheid 170, 180
Appiah, Kwame Anthony 47
  on identity 21–2, 23
art 46, 86, 111
  and activism 170, 201–2, 232
  immersion in 26
  of performance 68
  and self-identity 40
  spirituality and 41
  and power 81
  why it exists 40–1
  as witness 65

and the younger generation 82
see also culture; writing
astronomy 19
asylum laws 230
Auden, W. H. 56–7
Auschwitz concentration camp
183–4, 220

B
Baddiel, David 205
how human nature has followed us
online 197–8
online toxicity 197–9
curbing online abuse 198–9
Bailey, David 88
can photographs change the world
79
God and aliens 80
role of photography in culture 78
what photography tell us about the
world today 80
Balinese monkey chants 67–8
Ballmer, Steve 128–9, 164
on entrepreneurship 134
Bannon, Steve 269
Barrett, Justin 47
emergence of religion 33
Bates, Laura 205
feminism 186–7
message for the next generation
192
scale of sexism 187
beauty, aesthetic 42–3
Bell, Alexander Graham 61
belonging, sense of 17, 117
Berger, John 52
Betts, Alexander 237
scale of migration and refugee
movement 228–9
a world without borders 233
Biocon 144
Bird, Rt. Hon. Lord 205
eradication of poverty and the
government 172
birth control 189–90, 194
Black Thought 88
art and social change 57–8
art and the younger generation 82

Blackstone Group 100–1, 111–12
*Blind Orion Searching for the Rising
Sun* (N. Poussin) 51
Blumenthal, Heston 88
role of food in our culture 84–5
why food is so important to us
83–4
Bohr, Niels 37
Bollywood 74–8
border control 233–4
Bosnian War 217
Botha, President B. W. 180
Bourdieu, Pierre 177
brain-computer interfaces 32
brains, human 86
Branson, Richard 164
characteristics of a successful
enterprise 148
role of entrepreneurs in society
136
role of philanthropy 152
source of ideas 147
what is entrepreneurship 130–1
Brexit 250, 257–9, 273
Buffett, Warren 151
Burch, Tory 164
entrepreneurial characteristics 145
what is entrepreneurship 132
Bush, George W. 254–5
business culture 99–100
excellence in company culture
100–1
see also company culture
Butterfield, Stewart 164
message for future entrepreneurs
161

C
Cameron, David 256–7
Campbell, Alistair 274
referendums and democracy
256–7
return of right-wing and populist
movements 248–9
Cantacuzino, Marina 237
are some acts unforgiveable 220–1
forgiveness in place of revenge 221
capitalism 150

Carroll, Sean 47
  fundamentals of life and quantum
    mechanics 35–6
  philosophical implications of
    quantum mechanics 37
Case, Steve 129, 164
  common entrepreneurial mistakes
    150–1
  message for future entrepreneurs
    158
  role of entrepreneurs in society
    141
  what is entrepreneurship 133
Catmull, Ed 88
  role of storytelling 53–4
cave paintings 33, 41
chanting 67–8
chemical weapons 213–14
Chilcot inquiry 254
chimpanzees and great apes 39–40
China 244, 262
Chomsky, Noam 274
  free and democratic societies
    244–5
  influence of large corporations in
    society 263–4
  what drives foreign policy 254–5
Chopra, Deepak 47
  humanity's failure to access
    potential 43–4
Christianity 34, 190
Church, George 48
  what is 'life' 29
Churchill, Winston 242–3, 262–3
cinema *see* films and cinema
classical music 68, 70
climate change 216
Clinton, Bill 254
Clinton, Hillary 193–4
colonialism 178–9
commerce and film industry 73–4
commercial longevity 149
Common European Asylum System
  230
communities, companies as 154
company culture
  building high-performance teams
    101

building trust 103
changing behaviours 103–4
dismissing sleep 114–15
embedded values 102
excellence in 100–1
learning from adversity 116–17
togetherness in success and failure
  111–12
consciousness 38–9, 42
content management systems 14
contraception 189–90, 194
Coppola, Sofia 188
Corbyn, Jeremy 249
Covid-19 30, 111, 119, 173, 259
Craven, Philip 205
  message to those living with
    disabilities 175
  scale of discrimination against
    people with disabilities 173–4
  meaning of 'disability' 174–5
Crépeau, François 238
  improving refugees' situation
    232–3
Crowley, Dennis 164
  role of failure in entrepreneurship
    155–6
Cuban, Mark 124
  failure in leadership 107
  negotiation 106
culture 17, 51–3, 86–7
  art and social change 55–7
  and education 44
  food in 82–5
  genre as extension of 68–9
  poetry 56–61
  role of food in 84–5
  role of photography in 78–9
  storytelling 53–4, 58, 87
  see also art; company culture;
    film and cinema; food; music;
    storytelling; writing

D
de Gaulle, Charles 257
de Klerk, F. W. 205
  abolition of apartheid 180
  segregation and colonialism
    178–80

decision making 119–20
democracy 17, 240–2, 271–3
  balancing freedom and national
    security 266–7
  citizen involvement in political
    discourse 257–8
  consequences of a lack of public
    engagement and knowledge of
    democracy 258–9
  citizens understanding of
    government 245–6
  engaging society with government
    259
  growth of anti-European
    sentiment 255–6
  free and democratic societies
    244–5
  influence of large corporations
    263–4
  law and 264–6
  referendums 256–8
  return of right-wing and populist
    movements 246–53
  social role of education 45
  understanding power 260–3
  and foreign policy 254–5
  what it is 242–4
  why it matters 244
depression and anxiety 30, 59,
  112–13
desertification of land 216
Dias, Dexter 205
  on race 176–7, 202
disabilities, people with 170, 176
  scale of discrimination against
    173–4
  meaning of 'disability' 174–5
discrimination and injustice 17,
  168–71
  people with disabilities 173–6
  poverty 171–3
  see also gender discrimination;
    LGBT+ communities; racism
    and race
Dragon's Den 160
Ducasse, Alain 83
  role of food in culture 85
Dyson, James 162, 165

entrepreneurial characteristics 143
  message for future entrepreneurs
    156
  what is entrepreneurship 131
  role of entrepreneurs in society 137

E
Ebadi, Shirin 238
  conflict and violence 212–13
  is conflict ever justifiable 214
  message to the next generation 227
  relationship of culture / religion to
    conflict / peacebuilding 219
  why war exists 210
economic crisis (2007–08) 247,
  248–9
economics and war 210, 216
economy and education 44
Edict of Nantes 228
Edison, Thomas 150
education and learning 20, 43, 174,
  213, 246
  failure to accessing potential 43–4
  girls and global development 191
  role in society 44–5
Edwards, Jamal 164, 165
  message for future entrepreneurs
    158
Einstein, Albert 36
Eisenhower, David 271
Elders' Gro Harlem Brundtland 218
electoral systems 242, 244–5, 249
Elumelu, Tony O. 165
  characteristics of a successful
    enterprise 149
  message for future entrepreneurs
    158–9
  role of entrepreneurs in society
    138–9
Emin, Tracey 89
  power of art 81–2
entrepreneurs 128–36, 161–3
  characteristics of 143–5
  characteristics of successful
    enterprises 148–9
  common mistakes 150–1
  key drivers 139–40
  and philanthropy 151–4

role in society 136–42
role of failure 155–6
sources of ideas 147–8
entropy, law of 28–9
Erdoğan, Recep 252
Europe and migration/refugees 229, 230, 231, 234, 249
European Union 250, 251, 257, 259
see also Brexit
Euthyphro (Plato) 28
evolution 29, 39

F
failure, role of 107–10, 155–6
faith and religion *see* 'God'; religion and faith; spirituality
Farage, Nigel 248, 249, 250, 269
Farquhar, Scott 165
companies as communities 154
fascism *see* Holocaust; Nazis; populism and nationalism
Faye, Jean-Pierre 253
fear
conquering 31
exploitation of 199–200, 248–9
of failure 108, 109
feminism 186–7
Ferencz, Ben 235, 236, 238
message to the next generation 226
possibility of world peace 224
fiction and gender, sexual, racial narratives 63–4
films and cinema 27, 72
importance in our culture 72–3
in Indian culture 74–8
role as a mode of expression 73
Finland 210, 214–15
Floyd, George 170
food 82–3
role in culture 84–5
why is it so important 83–4
forgiveness 220–1
Formula One 109–10, 115–16
Fox Quesada, Vicente 274
advice for the next generation 269–70
citizen involvement in political discourse 257–8

return of right-wing and populist movements 247–8
Friedman, Stew 124
meaning of leadership 96
'FUD' 199–200

G
Gates, Bill 151, 190
Gates, Melinda 205–6
global education for girls 191
issues faced by women internationally 189–90, 191, 192–3
Gbowee, Leymah 206
international injustice against women 190
gender discrimination 23, 170–1, 184–5
feminism 186–7
international issues 189–91, 192–3
talking about sexism 185–6
scale of sexism 187
social media and self-image 188–9
genetics 32, 38
genre as extension of culture 68–70
George the Poet 89
poetry and social change 57
why we write 54
Giving Pledge charity 151
globalization 250, 251
'God' 28, 32, 80
Goodall, Jane 48
chimpanzees and great apes 39–40
Gormley, Antony 46, 48
why art exists 40–1
Grameen Bank 140
Grayling, A. C. 274
return of right-wing and populist movements 249–50
what is democracy 242–3
Greengrass, Paul 89
importance of film in our culture 72–3
Grylls, Bear 48
conquering fear 31
religion 34
Guantanamo Bay detention camp 266–7

H
Hadfield, Colonel Chris 124
 are leaders born or made 118–19
 leading with incomplete
  information 120–1
 failure in leadership 108–9
Haig, Matt 206
 impact of social media on mental
  health 199–200
Hamel, Gary 125
 redefining leadership 98–9
Harari, Yuval Noah 46, 48
 fears and hopes for humanity 31–2
 human sense of otherness 27–8
health and fitness 115
Heaney, Seamus 60
Henry, Patrick 56–7
Herman, Susan 274
 balancing freedom and national
  security 266–7
 law and democracy 265–6
high-performance teams 101
Hinduism 24–5, 82–3
Hirsch, Afua 206
 race and identity 177–8
 institutional response to racism
  181
Hitler, Adolf 248
Holocaust 170, 182–4, 220
Hsieh, Tony 125
 meaning of leadership 94–5
Huffington, Arianna 125
 sleep and business culture 114–15
Huguenots 228
human rights 195–6, 203, 211–12
 see also disabilities, people with
  discrimination and injustice;
  gender discrimination; LGBT+
  communities; racism and race;
  refugees
Hunt, Ruth 206
 sexuality and identity 194–5
hunter-gatherers 27, 83–4
Hussein, Saddam 254

I
identity 17, 19–21
 faith and religion 25–6
 finding our 22–3
 human sense of otherness 28–9
 labels 21–2
 many-worlds theory 37
 and occupation 24
 politics 22–3
 sexuality and 194–5
 shaping society 23
 why identities matter 21–2
Iliad (Homer) 61–2
Ilves, Toomas Hendrik 275
 growth of anti-European
  sentiment 255–6
immigration 249, 252
 see also refugees
In Place of War charity 18, 150,
 175–6, 208, 222
India 52, 136
individualism 117
Industrial Revolution 98, 114
innovation 133, 137, 144, 145, 148,
 157, 158, 244
International Criminal Court 184–5,
 226
iPhones 34
Iraq, War with 254–5
Irish Republican Army (IRA) 221

J
Jain, Naveen 165
 message for future entrepreneurs
  159
 role of entrepreneurs in society 141
Jamil, Jameela 206
 how to stay hopeful 193–4
 reduction of women to their
  appearance 188
 social media and self-image 188–9,
  193–4

K
Kapoor, Anish 46, 48
 life well lived 26–7
 why art exists 41–2
Kapur, Siddarth Roy 89
 cinema in Indian culture 75
 Indian cinema reflecting diversity
  76–7

role of music in Bollywood 77–8
Karan, Donna 165
role of entrepreneurs in society
142
Kasparov, Garry 275
advice for the next generation
268–9
why democracy matters 244
Kauffman, L. A. 206–7
advice for the next generation of
activists 202
why we need activism 200–1
Knill, Iby 207
Auschwitz experience and identity
183–4
importance of sharing Auschwitz
experiences 184
Kor, Eva 220–1
Kotter, John 92, 122–3, 125
changing behaviours 103–4

L
Lang Lang 89
the art of performance 68
genre as extension of culture 70
music as extension of language
71–2
language
importance in communication
62–3
key to humanity 40
music's relationship to 70–1
vocabulary 62
why we write 54
law and democracy 264–6
law of entropy 28–9
Le Pen, Marine 248, 249, 250, 269
leadership 17, 92–3, 122–3
are leaders born or made 118–19
leading with incomplete
information 119–22
essential characteristics 99
failure in 107–9
changing behaviours 103–4
negotiation 106
redefining 98
resilience in 113, 115–17
styles of 96–7

mean of leadership 94–6
meaning of power 104–5
see also company culture
Lean, David 73
learning / education *see* education
and learning
Lewis, Cecil 216
Lewis, Michael 275
citizens understanding of
government 245–6
re-engaging society with
government 259
Lewis, Scarlett and Jesse 221
LGBT+ communities 171, 194
persecution and human rights
195–6
sexuality and identity 194–5
Li, Robin 165
characteristics of a successful
enterprise 148–9
entrepreneurial characteristics 143
message for future entrepreneurs
156
philanthropy 152
role of entrepreneurs in society
136–7
sources of ideas 147
what is entrepreneurship 131
Lieu, Ted 275
return of right-wing and populist
movements 251–2
what is democracy 243
life
being alive 25
and meaning 30
fundamentals and quantum
mechanics 35–6
meaning and morality 28–9
music and the human experience
67
origin of 29–30
well lived 25–2
what is 'life' and feeling alive 29–30
literature *see* storytelling; writing
Loach, Ken 89
role of cinema as a form of
expression 73–4
what constitutes a great story 74

long-form content 14–15
Lord's Resistance Army 208

M
Mandela, Nelson 180
many-worlds theory 37
Martel, Yann 86–7, 89
  role of storytelling in our culture 58
  great writing 61–2
  why we write 55
  writing and ethical / social responsibility 65
  writing and other forms of culture 62–3
Mazumdar-Shaw, Kiran 166
  entrepreneurial characteristics 144
  what is entrepreneurship 132
McChrystal, General Stanley 125
  failure in leadership 108
  meaning of leadership 94
  power and leadership 104–5
McGowan, Rose 48, 168, 204, 207
  identity 24
  talking about sexism and racism 185–6
media and racism 181–2
media and sexism 185, 187
meditation 26, 109, 115–16
Mengele, Josef 220–1
mental health
  impact of lifestyle on 114
  impact of social media on 188–9, 193–4, 199–200
  see also depression and anxiety
#MeToo 24, 185
Microsoft 128–9
Middle Ages 52
Middle East 60, 66, 214, 243, 250, 252
military leadership 95, 99, 105, 108, 121–2, 123
Moby 90
  genre as extension of culture 68–70
  music and the human experience 67
  music's relationship to language 70–1

morality 28–9, 117
Motion, Andrew 90
  poetry and social change 56–7
multilateralism 222–3
music
  in Bollywood films 77
  and the human experience 67
  relationship to language 70–1
Mustard Tree charity 173
Myanmar 217–18
Myers, General Richard 125
  meaning of leadership 95
  power and leadership 105

N
Naím, Moisés 275
  influence of power 261–2
  what is power 260
Namibia 27, 180
nanotechnology 32
Narayana Murthy, N. R. 166
  characteristics of a successful enterprise 149
  entrepreneurial characteristics 145
  philanthropy 153
  what is entrepreneurship 132
  role of entrepreneur in society 137–8
nationalism *see* populism and nationalism
NATO (North Atlantic Treaty Organization) 224
Nazis 196, 220, 226, 236, 246
negotiation 106
Neill, Sam 49
  what is a life well lived 27
  finding joy 30
neo-liberalism 247
Netflix 100, 146
networking 145
Neves, José 166
  message for future entrepreneurs 157–8
  what is entrepreneurship 134–5
9/11 terrorist attacks 103, 266–7
Nobel Peace Prize 140, 218
Northern Ireland 217–18, 221
nostalgia 66–7

Novogratz, Jacqueline 125–6
 building trust 103
 redefining success 110–11
 style of leadership needed today
   96–7
 tension between opposing values
   117–18
Nuremberg trials 236

O
Obama, Barrack 245, 248, 258
Ohanian, Alexis 134
O'Leary, Kevin 166
 message for future entrepreneurs
   160
Otto, Michael 166
 philanthropy 153–4

P
Pakistan 255
Paralympians 174
Passarlay, Gulwali 238
 improving refugees' situation 231
peacebuilding / reconciliation
   217–23
Pearl Harbor attacks 181–2
Perry, Rick 246
Peterson, Jordan B. 49
 what is a life well lived 25–6
Petition of Right (1628) 268
philanthropy 151–4
philosophy and quantum mechanics
   36–8
photography
 and changing the world 79–81
 role in culture 78
 and understanding ourselves 79
Picasso 232
Pinker, Steven 49
 meaning of life and morality 28–9
Plato 28, 236
poetry 58–9, 111
 role in our culture 59–61
 and social change 56–8
populism and nationalism 224–5,
   235–6, 246–53, 256–7
positivism 36
possibilists 192–3

poverty 173
 changes over time 171–2
 role of the government in
   eradication 172, 173
power 260
 citizens understanding 261–3
 and leadership 104–5
Professor Green 124
 lifestyle and mental health 114
protests *see* activism

Q
quantum mechanics 35–8

R
racism and race 168–70, 176–7,
   185–6, 202–3, 216
 apartheid 170, 180
 colonialism 178–80
 media portrayal of race 181–2
 race and identity 177–8
 institutional response to 181
 see also discrimination and
   injustice
Rand, Ayn 204
Rankin 90
 can photographs change the world
   80–1
 photography and understanding
   ourselves 79
Reagan, Ronald 268
referendums 256–8
refugees
 countries' obligations to refugees
   230
 improving the situation for 231
 scale of migration and refugee
   movement 228–30
 sustainable migration 233
 a world without borders 233–4
Reich, Robert 126
 style of leadership needed today 97
religion and faith 21, 24–5, 27–8
 emergence of 33
 and war 216
 see also spirituality
renewable energy 147
resilience in leadership 113, 115–17

risk-taking 111–12, 130–1, 133, 134, 143
Robinson, Ken 49
  role of education in society 44–5
Rome statute 184–5
Rosberg, Nico 126
  building a high-performance team 101
  F1 skills applied in business 115–16
  meaning of success and failure 109–10
Rosling, Hans 192–3
Rovelli, Carlo 19, 49
  philosophical implications of quantum mechanics 37–8
Rumi 60
Rupp, George 238–9
  scale of migration and refugee movement 229–30
  a world without borders 234
Russia 224, 256–7
  see also Soviet Union

S
Saad, Gad 207
  courage to fight 201-2
Sadhguru 49
  being alive 25
  role of spirituality 34
Safina, Carl 50
  experience of consciousness 38–9
Sandberg, Sheryl 126
  learning from adversity 116–17
Sanders, Bernie 251–2
Sandy Hooke school massacre 221
Schwarzman, Stephen 126
  excellence in company culture 100–1
  togetherness in success and failure 111–12
second law of thermodynamics 28–9
Second World War 214, 226, 232, 236
  see also Holocaust
self-belief 158
sexism *see* gender discrimination
sexual harassment / abuse 185, 186–7
Shafak, Elif 50, 90
  identity politics 22–3

  narratives around gender, sexuality, race, etc. 63–4
  nostalgic writing 66
Shakespeare, William 56
Shark Tank television programme 106, 160
Shirreff, General Sir Richard 126
  leading with incomplete information 121–2
  essential characteristics of leadership 99
  meaning of leadership 95
Sidhwani, Ritesh 90
  Indian cinema reflecting diversity 76
  role of music in Bollywood 77
Sissay, Lemn 90
  poetry and social change 57
  role of poetry in our culture 59–60
sleep in company culture 114–15
Smith, Adam 263
Smith, Harry Leslie 207
  poverty over time 171
social change and writing 55–8
social class 23, 171–3
social conditioning 43
social media 64, 185, 188–9, 193–4, 197–200
social security 172
South Africa 178–80, 222
Soviet Union 180, 214–15
  see also Russia
Spanish Inquisition 177
spirituality
  and art 41
  the role of 34
  see also God; religion and faith
Star Trek 232
Starck, Philippe 50
  what is aesthetic beauty 42–3
Stavridis, Admiral James 275
  the influence of power on citizens 262–3
  what is power 260–1
storytelling 53–4, 74, 87
  narratives around gender, sexuality, race, etc. 63
  role in culture 53–4, 58

stress, lifestyle 114
success 109–11
Sudan 216
sustainable development 138, 149,
  158–9
sustainable migration 233
Sweden 223–4
Szostak, Jack 50
  what is 'life' and feeling alive 29–30

T
Takei, George 207
  media portrayal of race 181–2
Tatchell, Peter 203, 207
  hopes for the future 196–7
  human rights and LGBT+
    persecution 195–6
teamwork 101, 122–3, 159
Temelkuran, Ece 276
  return of right-wing and populist
    movements 246–7, 252–3
Terence 65
terrorism 266–7
texting 64
thermodynamics, second law of 28–9
Thought Economics blog 14–16
Thunberg, Greta 98
Toscani, Oliviero 80–1
Trump, Donald 198, 250–1, 252, 258,
  268–9
trust, importance of 103, 105, 210
truth in writing 61
Turkey 22, 66, 252
Twitter 198, 199

U
Uganda 208–9
UK foreign policy 254, 255
UKIP 248, 256
Ultima Group 13
Ulukaya, Hamdi 127
  company values 102
  role of business in society 122
United Nations 138, 180, 191, 195–6,
  222
United States of America 170, 181–2,
  223, 234, 244–6, 251–2, 254, 258,
  263–4, 266–7

universe, branching 37

V
values, tension between 117–18
Vanity Fair 146–7
Varoufakis, Yanis 240, 276
  advice for the next generation 269
Vaynerchuk, Gary 166
  what is entrepreneurship 135
Verhofstadt, Guy 273, 276
  advice for next generation 270
  consequences of a lack of public
    engagement and knowledge of
    democracy 258–9
  return of right-wing and populist
    movements 250–1

W
Wales, Jimmy 15
Wałęsa, Lech 235, 238–9
  forgiveness replacing revenge 221–2
  on conflict 215
  relationship of culture / religion to
    conflict / peacebuilding 220
  conflict in society 210–11
  message for the next generation
    224–5
war, peace and justice 208–10, 234–6
  applying peacebuilding techniques
    222–3
  are some act unforgiveable 220–1
  can conflict ever be justified
    213–15
  creating resilient peace 219
  forgiveness in place of revenge
    221–2
  fragility of global order 215–16
  conflict and violence as part of
    human nature 212–13
  key causes of conflict and war 216
  messages for the next generation
    225–7
  possibility of world peace 223–4
  refugees 228–34
  relationship of culture / religion to
    conflict / peacebuilding 220
  start of the peacebuilding process
    217–18

why does it exist 210–11
why peace breaks down 211–12
worries for the next generation
224–5
Warren, Earl 182
Weiwei, Ai 207, 232
advice for the next generation 202
art in political and social
conversation 201
moral and ethical responsibilities
of the artist 201
Welch, Jack 166
message for future entrepreneurs
159
what is entrepreneurship 133
Whyte, Jude 221
Wilde, Oscar 221
will.i.am 167
entrepreneurial characteristics 145
message for future entrepreneurs
159–60
role of entrepreneurs in society
141–2
Williams, Jody 235, 239
on conflict 213–14
key causes of conflict and war 217
possibility of world peace 223
Williams, Saul 90
role of poetry in our culture 60–1
Willink, Jocko 127
leading with incomplete
information 119–20
resilience in leadership 113
Wilson, Chip 167
entrepreneurial characteristics
143–4
role of entrepreneurs in society
140
role of failure in entrepreneurship
155
Wittgenstein, Ludwig 70–1
Woolf, Lord 276
balancing freedom and national
security 266–7
law and democracy 264–5
Woollard, Catherine 239
obligations to refugees 230
scale of migration and refugee

movement 229
a world without borders 233–4
writing
ethical / social responsibility 65
fictional narratives and sex,
gender, race issues 63–4
nostalgic 66
and other forms of culture 62–3
and social change 55–8
great writing 61–2
why we write 54–5
and youth culture 64

Y
Yang, Jerry 162, 167
common entrepreneurial mistakes
151
what is entrepreneurship 133
Youssef, Bassem 271, 276
advice for the next generation 268
what is democracy 243–4
youth culture 64
Yunus, Muhammad 128, 167
message for future entrepreneurs
157
philanthropy 152–3
role of entrepreneurs in society
137
what is entrepreneurship 131–2

Z
Zimmer, Hans 91
genre as extension of culture
69–70
music and the human experience
67–8
music as extension of language 71